Childless By Choice

The Meaning & Legacy
of a Childfree Life

Helen Taylor

الاسلام نور

DEDICATION

For my brothers Geoffrey and Richard Taylor
In memory of Ida Taylor
&
For Derrick Price
and all the relatives and friends in my extended family

First published in 2025 by
Helen Taylor, in partnership with Whitefox Publishing

www.wearewhitefox.com

Copyright © Helen Taylor, 2025

EU GPSR Authorised Representative
LOGOS EUROPE, 9 rue Nicolas Poussin, 17000,
LA ROCHELLE, France
E-mail: Contact@logoseurope.eu

ISBN 978-1-917523-30-1 (hardback)
Also available as an eBook
ISBN 978-1-917523-32-5

Designed and typeset by Typo•glyphix
Cover design by Heike Schüssler
Project management by Whitefox Publishing

Contents

Preface

In recent years, a debate has raged – usually among young women journalists and professionals – about the desirability of choosing to have children. Many books have been published with titles such as *The Baby Decision, Childfree and Loving It!*, *I'd Rather Get a Cat and Save the Planet: Conversations with Childfree Women*, and *Women Without Kids: The Revolutionary Rise of an Unsung Sisterhood*. The debate focuses on the problem of finding the right partner with whom to procreate; the time bomb of entering middle age with weaker fertility and energy; the assault childbearing makes on your body, time, income and promotion prospects; and the chutzpah to bring a child into a world of climate emergency, overpopulation, and a cost-of-living crisis precipitated by war. All of this is discussed in terms of 'choice' – a word that is always important in any debate in a capitalist society of about lifestyle or life directions, and that is usually now associated with those affluent enough to have a range of options. There is a growing industry in books and podcasts offering advice, often from American sources – such as wealth specialist Jay Zigmont's *The Childfree Guide to Life and Money*.

I am a woman in her seventies who never wanted children. I am stepmother to a German man and step-grandmother to his four Danish children, aunt to my brothers' three children and my partner's three nieces, as well as great-aunt to seven. But no one has ever called me Mummy or Granny, I have never been a godmother, I've never read aloud *We're Going on a Bear Hunt*, and I am what is commonly described as 'childless by choice'. I am of an age and generation that generally had children, so people always assume I'm a mother, and more. Whenever I buy presents for friends' or relatives' children's children, the shop assistant will comment on 'those lucky grandchildren'. When I see harassed mothers and grandparents, they smile at me with recognition. 'You know what we're going through,' they think. And although I can well imagine it – no, I really don't.

'Choice' has, however, always been a key term in feminist parlance. 'A woman's right to choose' was a mantra of the second-wave women's movement – especially in terms of contraception and abortion, at a time when those rights were under constant attack and often hard to obtain. I am acutely aware that I am a member of the first generation to benefit from medical and technological advances and have been able to 'choose' whether or not to procreate. Following the life-changing development of the contraceptive pill and the liberalisation of abortion laws in western countries, including the 1967 Abortion Act in the UK and the 1973 *Roe v. Wade* ruling in the US, women's right to choose seemed confirmed. However, the ability to choose has since been undermined over the decades with growing attacks on abortion – most dramatically, the United States Supreme Court's 2022

Dobbs v. Jackson Women's Health Organization reversal of *Roe v. Wade*, and threats to access to contraception. In his second term of office, President Trump's determination to limit or abolish abortion has ominous echoes of Hitler's decision to close all clinics and declare abortion a crime against the state. In many countries, contraception and abortion are impossible or very difficult to obtain. This is a class issue, too. Across the world, the higher the literacy rate, the lower the birth rate.

'Choice' NOT to reproduce assumes many things. First, you come from a social or religious group which neither proscribes birth control nor sees motherhood as a woman's primary role. Next, you are prepared to resist our culture's pro-natalist discourse and the popular conflation of womanhood with motherhood. You have a sympathetic partner or social group who agree with or tolerate your decision. You aren't living with someone who rapes you and/or forbids the use of reliable contraception. You can take the disapproval or bewilderment of family and friends at your 'selfish' 'unnatural' decision. Finally, you have interesting alternative life possibilities if the status of parent isn't granted you. Non-parents tend to be white, highly educated, urban, non-religious, and concentrated in professional and managerial occupations. Rarely does the choice of the women of developing countries and working-class women of racial and ethnic minorities, as well as LGBTQ+ women, become part of the debate. Such women often have few choices and advantages, and face greater social pressures. Pregnancy can be the inevitable result of deprivation and poverty, or a conveyor of status on a woman who has little power or agency.[1]

I've been thinking a lot about the question of 'choice', especially since watching on Zoom Duncan Macmillan's 2011 play *Lungs*, now seen as more relevant than ever since it's a prolonged debate between a white middle-class heterosexual couple about whether or not to have a baby. Reflecting on his play eight years after its debut, Macmillan wrote:

> The things that felt most absurd or satirical – that a couple would factor in climate change into their decision whether or not to become parents, for example – have become less laughable. At the time of writing it seemed that these overthinking, self-conscious liberal characters were using the uncertainty of the future as a way to avoid making the commitment. But now their concerns feel more sincere and echo those I hear in conversations with friends. Climate Change doesn't feel so far away or abstract. The world seems more politically volatile. The future is uncertain.[2]

In a 2020 study published in the journal *Climatic Change*, surveying six hundred Americans aged 27–45 (largely white, well-educated, liberal), researchers found that 96 per cent were concerned about 'the wellbeing of their future children in a climate-changed world' and they worried about the carbon footprint of children producing a lifetime of carbon emissions. Often expressed in emotionally charged terms, the study was peppered with fears of apocalyptic change. One respondent said the impact of global heating would 'rival World War One in its sheer terror'. One woman decided not to have biological children because 'I don't want to birth children into a dying world [though] I dearly want to be a mother'. The lead researcher even found that 6 per cent of parents confessed to remorse about having children, with some mentioning a fear that their children will face the end of the world.

It seems the young on both sides of the Atlantic are factoring climate change into their considerations of reproduction. Matthew Schneider-Mayerson, Associate Professor of Environmental Studies at Rice University in Houston, Texas, even claims 'scores of women' in the UK have started a 'birth strike' until the climate crisis is resolved. The fact that the planet may end lets a woman off the hook, and gives a moral power to her decision – but it also closes down debate or nuanced consideration. As Eva Wiseman says, 'these doom-tinged prophecies are not unique to those with climate anxiety – they are baked into parenthood . . . There are thousands of reasons not to have kids – the fact that the world is ending is simply one of them.' She challenges the somewhat cerebral notion of a 'choice' by comparing procreation with falling in love: 'This is what humans do. And each child's future will always be uncertain, because that is the nature of future.' She also argues constructively that having a baby can 'radicalise' a person, 'creating a family determined to improve their planet's future'.[3]

American writer Meehan Crist challenges the idea that reproduction is a matter of personal choice while global fossil fuel companies greenwash their carbon footprint and fail to challenge the climate disaster facing the planet. She argues that such major structural change is required that personal choice is irrelevant (and she chose to give birth).[4] It was perhaps more difficult for women to justify having children at a time of international crisis when Putin's war on Ukraine was posing an immediate threat to the world's energy supplies, leading to 'the cost-of-living crisis'. Poverty doesn't usually prevent pregnancy, but the scale of this crisis may well have made many a woman (and their partners) think twice. As will the new challenges and threats of AI, which some commentators suggest may utterly transform – or bring about the end of – the world.

The terms 'childless' and 'childfree', which I'll use throughout this book, are never neutral. 'Childless' suggests loss, inadequacy and sorrow; actor Kim Cattrall famously described the 'less' as offensive, sounding as if *you* are less because you haven't had a child. On the other hand, 'childfree' sounds smug and complacent, and perhaps a little sad. The chilling term 'barren' has no masculine equivalent, and no one talks about a 'childless man' or 'non-fathers'.

Every woman has her own story about having or not having children, and for each one there are problematic and sometimes heartrending issues and circumstances. Many childless women – the 'bunch of childless cat ladies' made famous by Vice President J. D. Vance – have tragic stories of miscarriage ('baby loss'), failed IVF, enforced abortion or adoption, illness or infertility preventing conception, and so on, all of which blight lives. For others, who may have experienced some of the same things, later life brings a reconciliation to and even relief about their childless/free state. A final group may have jumped through many of the hoops encountered in a reproductive life, and feel nothing but quiet pleasure that they remain childfree.

For the majority of women, it seems, the specifics of their private stories are closely guarded, rarely aired with friends or acquaintances. That said, while this delicate subject used to be not spoken about or only alluded to indirectly, in the last few years the media, women's magazines and businesses have become alert to the sensitivity of those who are childless, have lost family members, or have had terrible life experiences around (in)fertility. In recent times, several online businesses have emailed offering me flowers, chocolates or sexy lingerie for Mother's Day, then apologised if they'd upset me, giving me the chance to opt out of publicity.

No need. My tale is not tragic – though it contains bewilderment, regret and sorrows, as well as happiness and fulfilment. I had an illegal abortion that was performed safely by a Harley Street doctor, and to my relief no more pregnancies (helped by sterilisation in my early forties). I have had two relationships involving stepchildren whom I found challenging but not monstrous. Most significantly, my long-term partner has expressed no desire to father a child with me. That said, there are doubts and ambivalences I have never really confronted, and for the sake of younger women and my contemporaries who share such feelings, I'm going to try to unpack them in the following pages.

Chapter 1

Why I Chose
a Childfree Life

A classic baby boomer, I was born in 1947, two years after the end of World War II, and grew up as the National Health Service, the Butler Education Act and post-war peace and prosperity transformed family and individual lives. I'm part of a blessed generation that escaped a major war and had access to free healthcare, good schooling and grant-aided higher education – and was one of the earliest groups to be offered the contraceptive pill. Now envied or resented by younger generations, I secured a safe, steady teaching job which – though offering a modest salary – enabled me to get a mortgage and move relatively seamlessly into the middle class.

I was raised in a lower-middle-class home that was busy and fraught. I am the middle child between two very gifted and feisty brothers. Neither of my parents had been to college or university, and money was tight. My mother, who had extraordinary drive and self-discipline, did most things in the house and garden while also working part-time, while my father – supposedly the main breadwinner – was a paint salesman in a precarious world where you lost your job at the drop of a hat (or dropping sales figures). His excuse for minimal domestic and childcare involvement came from all the travelling he had to do and the social life he claimed he needed to keep up with customers (the latter involving a lot of golf and alcohol). I remember few intimate conversations with him, though he was a handsome and charming man who drove me everywhere I needed to go – school, the bus station, teenage parties. He smoked non-stop – this finally killed him – and I remember with some distress sitting in a smoke-filled car with the windows closed, so I was very often carsick. He spoke little at home, his wife and three children filling all possible silences, and he seemed to relish sitting alone in our lounge watching TV or snoozing gently.

I now realise, with the generosity hindsight can give you, that he was very depressed. He was a gifted man whose distinguished wartime army career had ended disastrously, and this badly affected his marriage and family relationships. My mother was an intelligent but sad and bitter woman, who – because her sister's ill health resulted in huge pre-NHS medical bills – was forced to work in a Bolton tannery instead of going to college. She had three children when she would happily have remained with one, and was unable to return to education until late in her life. She worked in secretarial jobs for many years, but finally retrained as a teacher of commercial subjects, then special-needs children. She always seemed exhausted, and it's not surprising when I think of the sheer drudgery of domestic work for that generation. We had few domestic appliances (a mangle for the washing, no fridge, freezer or microwave, and no central heating so fires had to be lit daily).

She kept reminding me – in terms that I now see were fairly hurtful – that children were a burden and a problem, and if I were wise I would never have any. A dutiful, but never doting, grandmother to my brothers' children, she often told me how irritating it was in later life that other bowls club members talked of nothing but their ailments and their grandchildren. A woman of broad interests, she didn't see herself as being at the heart of an extended family (and thus having to spend even more time in the kitchen). Not for her the hand-knitted jumpers and toys, the special cakes for children's birthdays, and the long holidays *en famille*.

Unlike my friends, my brothers and I didn't have a cat or dog upon which to shower childish love, but we did have dolls and teddies. Although never interested in real babies and toddlers, I was devoted to my dolls, and my mother and I used baby voices to give the dolls characterful speech. At the age of three, I spent several weeks in hospital with scarlet fever, my parents unable to visit, and I was forbidden to take in my dolls because of cross-infection. When I came out, ecstatic to be reunited with my dolls, my parents playfully arranged a wedding between my favourite, Angela, and my brother's Teddy. My father drove them round the block, followed by a ceremony in our lounge and a special tea for everybody. I was a devoted and fussy mother to Angela and Eileen and remember my powerful maternal feelings for them. They suited me well, since I didn't have to change nappies or feed them, and I could exert complete control over their movements and moods in the knowledge that they would suffer no adverse emotional consequences. Both my dolls were so cheaply made that over the years the stuffing fell out of them; I'm touched to recall that my parents sent them to the dolls' hospital for repair. Angela never looked the same after her cosmetic surgery, and some years later her head fell off. I still have my decapitated girl sitting in a box; I can't bear to throw her away.

Until my mid- to late-teenage years, I was extremely close to and inordinately influenced by my mother (something I now realise has lasted much of my life, even after her death). When I lived at home, she and I would sit for hours at the kitchen table, where she'd tell me of her aspirations and thwarted ambitions, while encouraging me to live a childfree life that – in her terms – would be blissfully unproblematic. She saw education as the solution for everything and believed that going to university and becoming a teacher would give me the life she never had. I remember her saying wistfully that higher education would solve all our problems, though she later came to understand this was not the case. We never discussed sexuality, a subject about which – as a teenager – I was obsessed. She couldn't acknowledge to me – even though she knew instinctively – that her daughter would be in thrall to the joys and complexities of sexual desire in an extremely patriarchal society. This issue pushed us apart, and I went my own way. When she discovered I'd lost my virginity at a party, she expressed deep disappointment – probably because she knew what was coming next . . . In her book about her own childlessness, *Motherhood*, Sheila Heti suggests she might have been born with her mother's 'ball of grief or sorrow or negativity', which is 'gnawing at' her.[1] All my life I've felt I was compensating for, or struggling to escape from, that same ball.

Passing the eleven-plus exam, I went to a girls' grammar school in Birmingham. As at all such elite schools at the time, we were taught largely by single women whom we both admired and pitied. The common explanation for the 'spinsters' was that their fiancés had been killed in World War II. In other words, they had loved and lost, though we often suspected many of them had never loved at all. Single women over thirty – which was old to us schoolgirls – seemed to have had no life experience, and we wondered what they did in the long evenings and weekends after school. The term 'spinster' was almost always used derogatorily or dismissively, and we all knew we didn't want to be one of those. When an engagement ring appeared on a teacher's finger, her glamour quotient went up considerably; while the ones who dressed in a fairly masculine fashion were assumed to be lesbian (even if we didn't really know what that meant). The married ones seemed like proper grown-ups, especially if they had children, and a teacher whose pregnancy began to show was a subject of gossip and awe. We assumed that having a baby would end a teacher's career. She often left her job as the pregnancy developed and then would turn up at school with the new baby, showing it off to teachers and girls alike. That would be the last we saw of her and we never speculated about what happened to her after the birth.

Our teachers all encouraged us to study hard and go on to higher education, but the most repeated advice was that you should do a postgraduate teacher training course, then take up a teaching post which would fit in with marriage and give you school holidays to spend with your children. However, the most charismatic single, childless science teacher was an ambitious and beautiful woman who pooh-poohed all that and invited my friends and me to her oh-so-gorgeous flat where her lover dropped in (no 'spinster' she). That was my sort of life, I decided.

As I became part of that boomer generation later associated with 'the sixties', I wanted to get away from all that my parents represented, including what seemed a dreary notion of 'family'. I left home to study in London, then the US, and on my return I never really went back. I felt uncomfortably alienated from my parents, who had seemed in my adolescence to share few of my interests or values (especially around politics, romantic love and sex). Unfair though I now realise that was, I had felt constrained by a household of five people who endlessly squabbled, talked about football, and required too much washing-up and ironing when all I wanted was to read books and dream about the pop stars and boys I fancied. My parents often said they had three 'only children', and it's true that, in our childhood, we didn't share a great deal (though in later life we have moved very much closer). As I've grown older, I marvel at my friends' children who have developed informal friendships with their parents, sharing political and cultural views and experiences, and are invited to sleep with partners in the parental home. Family lives have certainly become less puritanical and prescriptive.

When I was thirty, I got together with a partner who shared my scepticism about all that 'family' and 'generations' meant. It was a long time before we introduced each other to our parents, and then had somewhat distanced relations with them – until they became ill in older age. We both then fell into line, dutifully and affectionately attending to them until the end. I remember my mother saying, while disabled and depressed in a residential home, that my brothers and I were the only people with whom she felt comfortable, and the only reason she was staying alive. Meanwhile she exacted many a practical task of me at a time when I was in one of the most demanding jobs of my life. When she said how lucky I was to have no children to worry about, I said to her, 'But unlike you, I'll never have a daughter for me to feel comfortable with.' I didn't add that I might feel there was no reason for me to stay alive. This was when I was in my fifties, possibly the first time I had twinges of regret for having chosen a childless route.

After I retired from teaching in order to write books and curate literary festivals, my partner and I went to Corsica for a fortnight's holiday. We rented an apartment during school term-time and set out daily along the beach to a quiet spot where we read, ate and swam. To my consternation, I began to focus on family groups – often of French parents, grandparents and young children – gently enjoying time together, picnicking, playing on the sand, venturing into the water. I kept seeing Impressionist tableaux of attractive women in glamorous garb, children in cute bathing suits and outfits, and sun-kissed grandparents looking on and giving a helping hand. To my shocked surprise, I sensed what I had missed, and what my friends had meant when they said they wanted children. That was a turning point; from then on, I began to notice how beautiful and charming children can be, and what magical fun they can provide for adults.

That sounds absurdly schmaltzy. I didn't come home an emotional wreck. I think it just made me aware of the limitations of my choice and the narrow range of my human interactions. I didn't really want that beach scenario for myself – I was happy to admire it at a distance. The whole paraphernalia of a life of different generations; the amount of sheer stuff you have to cart around to keep children well and happy; the chaos and untidiness of people of different ages, tastes and habits; the cacophony of voices and different conversational styles – these have always rather disturbed me. Of all things in life, I've treasured solitude, silence, time and space for reading, walking, films and music, gardening and pottering, as well as precious intimacy with my partner. Groups of mixed generations – which many people see as giving their life profound joy and meaning – sometimes delight and amuse me, but all too often exhaust or stifle me. That said, I'm aware that often those mixed generations drive one another crazy, and exhaustion and a feeling of being stifled are not exclusive to childless women like me.

Pregnancy and Abortion

As a first-year English student in London, I fell deeply in love with Geoff, who was reading law. Both of us lived in university halls of residence, so meeting and having sex was a cloak-and-dagger affair – smuggling each other into halls and making out on narrow single student beds. I got pregnant the third time we made love (a split condom donated by Geoff's best friend). It was the summer term, and I was acting in a student production of John Osborne's *Look Back in Anger*, the first night of which coincided with my visit to the student health centre to do a pregnancy test. Because my periods were very regular, I was certain I must be pregnant, but the kind nurse told me the result was negative and gave me a sedative so I could act in the play and afterwards spend time with my proud parents, who'd come from Birmingham to watch me. I was told to return two weeks later; by then the test was positive. I phoned Geoff the morning of his first law exam and used my acting skills to assure him the whole thing was a false alarm, and he should sit his exam with a light heart. He didn't believe me, but he did pass the exam.

This was 1967, cruelly just a couple of months before David Steel's abortion bill passed through Parliament, making abortion legal under certain conditions. I had no conversations with fellow students or friends about termination, except for two Catholic young men with whom I worked at Wimbledon serving strawberry teas during the tennis fortnight. Steel's bill was in the news, and they both casually talked about his advocacy of murder. The guilt, shame and terror my youthful pregnancy produced in me were calmed by the courageous support of the university health service. Familiar with this pre-pill disaster – more than one girl in my hall of residence had sat in a hot bath with gin in an attempt to dislodge the foetus

– a nurse discreetly advised me to say to the doctor who would refer me for an abortion that, if the pregnancy proceeded, I would kill myself. Again, with my acting skills, this is what I did. He duly signed the forms and I got my abortion, administered by a sympathetic Harley Street doctor and costing us £60 – a huge sum at the time for penniless students.

The worst part of it was that, being under twenty-one (the age of consent at the time), I had to get my parents' written permission. Since my boyfriend and I had planned to go through the process without involving them, and had arranged a place to stay so I could recover, this was a blow indeed. I took the coach home to Birmingham, sat at the kitchen table and confessed to my horrified parents, who urged us to marry at once (we refused) and insisted I come home immediately after the operation. What I didn't know at the time was that my mother had undergone an illegal abortion after her fourth pregnancy, and had assumed her university student daughter would be immune from such a fate. The shame of either unmarried pregnancy or an abortion, as well as the unwelcome memories this clearly stirred up in my mother, was written all over their faces. After the operation, they loyally drove to London, collected me and took me home. The subject was never mentioned again.

Like many young, confused women at a time when contraception for single women was difficult to obtain and abortion still illegal, I felt huge guilt about taking the step I did, and for a long time afterwards was deeply depressed. I even spoke to one of my middle-aged male tutors – who was flustered and embarrassed but did let me off an essay deadline.

My relationship, which had been so sweet, floundered, and I took up with another man with whom I refused to have sex. Years later, I saw my ex-boyfriend Geoff, who admitted it had been traumatic for him, too, but he confirmed my certainty that at the time we were too young and impoverished, and having a baby would have ruined our degree courses, our careers and probably our relationship. He went on to marry and have two daughters. I envied the way that – after our traumatic joint experience – he could enjoy (as I saw it) an unproblematic family life.

Would that I had read more women's fiction at the time. In Carol Dyhouse's history of post-war love and sexuality, *Love Lives: From Cinderella to Frozen* (2021), she notes how many novels of the 1950s and early 1960s about female students – by writers such as Penelope Mortimer, Rona Jaffe and Andrea Newman – end not in marriage but with miserable abortions.[2] This makes me recall those trailblazing films about premarital sex and abortion which don't end well – *Room at the Top* (1959), *Saturday Night and Sunday Morning* (1960), *Alfie* (1966), and more recently Mike Leigh's retrospective study of a 1950s abortionist, *Vera* (2004).

Artists and writers have long participated in the abortion debate. In 1998, the year of the first referendum debate on abortion in Portugal, artist Paula Rego produced ten large paintings set in backstreet abortion clinics, depicting vividly the horror and suffering of desperate women. She made etchings of her series, *Untitled: The Abortion Pastels*, so they could be widely distributed. Published in Portuguese newspapers in 2007 before a second referendum, they are said to have contributed strongly to the vote's success. In 2022, when I saw this series exhibited in a special room at Bristol's Arnolfini Gallery, I was almost physically sick, then haunted for days by the paintings' uncompromising power. I recalled *A Spark of Light*, Jodi Picoult's 2018 novel about a gunman's attack on the only abortion clinic in Mississippi, including debates about when life begins, whose life matters most, and how biopolitics works against African-American women in a white supremacist project. The wounded African-American abortion doctor, Ward, addresses the central issue: 'Whether or not you believed a fetus was a human being, there was no question in anyone's mind that a grown woman was one.'[3]

The French writer and Nobel Prize winner Annie Ernaux published *Happening* (2022), a powerful memoir of her illegal abortion in 1963, recounting the lonely and painful experience she had trying to get help from a doctor and then going to a backstreet abortionist who brought on a miscarriage that could have killed her. The matter-of-fact narrative and lack of self-dramatisation or self-pity make her story all the more moving, especially as she concludes by claiming to have put into words 'an extreme human experience, bearing on life and death, time, law, ethics and taboo'.[4] Since her illegal abortion in Paris predated mine in London by only four years, this resonated and reminded me that – had I not been treated by an enlightened student health centre – I too could have ended up with a dangerous backstreet operation.

In the years that followed my abortion, like other women with whom I've discussed this, I often found myself wondering about the child I never had. A married friend recently told me she often dreams of the baby she had aborted after having two healthy children – realising she didn't think she could cope with another. For some reason I've never understood, I was certain I was going to have a boy, and I often fantasise about the man he would have become. What would he have been like, and what would he have done with his life? Would he have loved me, and become an intellectual as well as an emotional companion? Or hated me and run off to another continent as soon as he could? Would he blame me for getting pregnant so young and irresponsibly, or would the fact I was a young mother work in my favour? Would he have had children, and would he be there at my deathbed?

A Woman's Right to Choose?

For many years, I thought the slogan of second-wave feminism – 'a woman's right to choose' – so self-evident that most people, apart from religious fundamentalists, accepted it. However, in recent years, as feminism has come under attack from many quarters, multiple events have brought home to me the urgency of fighting a battle I thought we'd won. These events have also underlined how choosing to be a mother is far from the fluffy private and personal choice that many commentators suggest, and is always determined by urgent social and economic factors. Getting pregnant is one of the most politically charged and significant things a woman can do, and claiming a right over her body – to give birth or not – one of the most provocative.

If feminists relied on twentieth-century legal victories, we were certainly shaken out of our complacency on 24 June 2022, when the US Supreme Court (comprising nine people, five male and five Catholic) overturned *Roe v. Wade*, the 1973 legislation that made access to abortion a federal right in the United States. The decision, undoing fifty years of legal protection, paved the way for individual states to curtail or ban abortion rights. Probably inspired by this, after the election of Giorgia Meloni's neo-fascist Brothers of Italy party, an Italian senator was encouraged to bring forward an amendment to Italy's civil code that would classify pregnancy terminations as murder. In Thailand and Ireland, where abortion was recently decriminalised (in 2021 and 2019 respectively), restrictions remain, and several women took action in the European Court of Human Rights after January 2021, when Poland criminalised abortion in almost all circumstances.

How can we ever forget that image of President Trump's first day in the White House in January 2017, surrounded by senior white men, signing into law a presidential directive prohibiting federal funding for international organisations that promote or pay for abortions without espousing Christian conservative ideology? This led to thousands of deaths in the poorest countries. And it's not just women in the developing world. In 2009, the abortion doctor Dr George Tiller, who argued 'Trust women', was murdered in a Kansas church by an anti-choice militant.

The 2022 Supreme Court decision resulted in several US states immediately imposing significant restrictions on abortion. How shocking it was to see the lack of compassion by pro-life politicians and activists for abortion doctors and very young girls and women forced after rape or incest to bear babies or travel to pro-abortion states to get terminations. Feminists angrily claimed that anti-abortion laws were designed not to reduce foetal deaths, but to remind women that our function is to devote ourselves to childbearing, sanctified and policed by the state. The role of men as impregnators is never addressed (don't they deserve punishment too?), and the fact that women can enjoy non-reproductive sex as much as men appears to be too appalling to contemplate. During the 2024 presidential election, Donald Trump and his vice presidential candidate, J. D. Vance, both argued that abortion and IVF should be illegal, and talked erroneously about babies being aborted after birth. The Democratic candidate Kamala Harris challenged them to name one piece of legislation designed to restrict the male body. Silence.

A month after the US Supreme Court ruling, the *London Review of Books* devoted a large chunk of the 21 July 2022 edition to the personal testimonies of thirty women. Elif Batuman summarised the tone of the articles well. Speaking of her native Italy: '[T]here is nothing more political than the depoliticisation of the lives of women and children. This ... effected on a wide scale, has now empowered a supposedly democratic state to force children to be born whom nobody, least of all the state itself, is equipped to love.'[5] Edna Bonhomme quoted an estimate that 41 per cent of people of childbearing age in the US would lose access to their nearest abortion clinic, involving travel of hundreds of miles to reach a provider in another state.

And UK women cannot afford to be complacent. There have been parliamentary challenges to abortion rights, with MP Danny Kruger claiming he doesn't believe women have 'an absolute right to bodily autonomy'. Alas, how right he is; abortion is still technically illegal. The 1967 Abortion Act didn't repeal the 1861 Offences against the Person Act; it simply outlined exceptions to the 1861 prohibition and handed to doctors the power to access each abortion's legality. In November 2022, there was a petition calling for UK abortion rights to be written up into the new Bill of Rights. A senior MP, Catholic Jacob Rees-Mogg, referred in Parliament to abortion as 'a cult of death'. As Arianne Shahvisi succinctly puts it, 'The same people who cannot be trusted regarding the uses of their bodies are trusted to raise a child.' Punchily, she adds: 'Unwanted pregnancy is forced labour.'[6] It's not difficult to see the link between 'pro-life' hostility towards women seeking to abort and those intent on remaining childfree. The notion of 'pro-life' has hijacked the notion of life, in contrast with the supposed 'pro-death' pregnancy-refusers. In 2024, a parliamentary bill proposing decriminalisation was scrapped because of an early general election.

I've dwelled at length on the abortion issue because for me it clarifies the dangers for women of daring to claim rights over their own bodies – indeed over their very physical autonomy. We can't be trusted not to 'get ourselves pregnant', and we certainly can't be trusted to take the matter into our own hands via abortion. Indeed, abortion itself is seen as a dark art practised by wise women, deviant women and of course witches (called 'weyward' by novelist Emilia Hart). It isn't surprising that a recent trend in women's fiction is 'witcherature', with novels such as Madeline Miller's *Circe* (2018) and Kirsty Logan's *Now She is Witch* (2023). 'Witch lit' has stories of marginalised, often eccentric, isolated women who have magical powers in relation to childbirth and abortion – while having no children of their own. In the post-Me Too and *Roe v. Wade* reversal period, writers and readers are turning to this mythical figure, who has been reconfigured as a feminist patriarchy-challenging icon existing outside the norm. But unlike the pointed-hat cat lady of childhood stories, she may be seductive, sorcerous, enchanting. In the musical and film *Wicked* (2024), a revisiting of *The Wizard of Oz*, we see a nuanced and witty contemporary version of witchcraft.

Historians explain the medieval and post-medieval European persecution of witches as a reaction to single, older, financially independent, menopausal childless women associated with pacts, covens and deadly powers. This has informed historical novels such as Beth Underdown's *The Witchfinder's Sister* (2017), about the 1645 Manningtree witch trials, and those by Stacey Halls and Elizabeth Lee about the 1612 Pendle witch trials, *The Familiars* (2019) and *Cunning Women* (2021). Childless women, especially those who are childfree by choice, are often seen as modern witches (crazy cat ladies and so on) – dangerous outsiders exerting dark powers over others. No wonder women choosing to remain childfree still feel they are the object of deep suspicion and thus fear they may be persecuted. On BBC *Woman's Hour*, distinguished academic and broadcaster Professor Mary Beard (who has long white hair and eschews fashionable dress) described tweets calling her an old witch. Wryly, she wondered 'what women over childbearing age are for'. The notion of the 'witch' recurs in many discussions of childlessness or childfreeness. Perhaps we older childless women should reclaim the name with defiance and pride – in Ruby Warrington's words, a 'Woman In Total Control of Herself'.

Other People's Children

My abortion and subsequent trauma didn't translate into a deep interest in other people's children, and I'm ashamed to say that I've often avoided picking up babies and playing with toddlers. Unlike all those women who gaze into prams to admire the baby, I focus on the face of the mother to see how she's coping. I like grown children, largely because I can relax into conversation with them and treat them like – well – adults. I was never a very playful child, and always wanted to be an adult; this means that other people's little kids undoubtedly find me either boring or a little frightening. Watching the film *Nomadland* (2020), I identified completely with the discomfort of childless protagonist Fern when her would-be lover handed her his baby granddaughter for a few minutes. The baby squirmed on her unwelcoming lap, and she panicked at the thought of having to deal with this alien creature. That could well have been me.

On the other hand, I would echo Sheila Heti's view that it is hard *not* to be a mother to anyone. The world is full of needy people who seek the nurture and sustenance they received or yearned for from their mothers, and throughout my adult life – with variable success – I've mothered family members, friends, students, colleagues, and sometimes even strangers. I've sent money to charities for mothers across the globe, and I've defended fraught women in public places when others have denounced crying babies and nuisance toddlers. I smile at mothers and grandmothers exhaustedly pushing strollers in the rain – and invariably receive a grateful look as they mistakenly identify me as one of them.

The game changer in my life was the Women's Liberation Movement, which was taking off in 1970 at the time I was studying for an MA and teaching in Baton Rouge, Louisiana – hardly a radical hotspot. I fell upon Betty Friedan's *The Feminine Mystique*, which illuminated my entire life as a young woman. Its angry, uncompromising account of women's domestic trials and professional disadvantage helped me understand some of my mother's unhappiness. I participated in groups, attended National Organization for Women conferences, and listened to women articulating deep dissatisfactions and desires about being female. It was a great time to be alive and in the United States, where the excitement and energy of the Black, gay and women's movements were transforming political and social discourse and action. I returned to the UK thoroughly radicalised and full of feminist ideas and self-righteousness.

I got my first teaching job at Bristol Polytechnic (now the University of the West of England) and joined the burgeoning women's movement in that city. In the early days of polytechnics (which had been established in the late sixties), many of our students on newly designed degree courses were 'mature' – having already worked for many years and/or raised families. All were thirsty for new ideas and ways of living, and the female (as well as a few enlightened male) students flocked to the Women's Studies courses some colleagues and I set up against stiff managerial opposition. They were eager to make sense of their past lives and the transformations they wished to make in the future. It was a heady time, and we believed we were changing the world and transforming gender roles.

Very quickly, I became a member of three groups: in Bristol, a consciousness-raising group and a collective writing group that produced the first Women's Studies textbook, *Half the Sky: An Introduction to Women's Studies* (1979); in London, a Marxist feminist literature group. The latter, which accepted me as a member despite my not identifying as Marxist, produced a paper for a university conference in 1978. As with the Bristol writing group, all of us went on to become published authors and academics, many with distinguished careers. I loved that exhilarating sense of being part of a new politics and lifestyle: 'Not the church and not the state, women must decide their fate!' Marriages and partnerships shifted, broke up, and new sexualities were explored. Having no intention of marrying, I enthusiastically supported the campaign group YBA Wife? (Why Be a Wife?), 1975–1984, which raised awareness of the discrimination married women faced in areas such as income tax, pension, social security and more. For me, the campaigns and writings of the Women's Liberation Movement came at just the right time, reinforcing my determination to live an emancipated life bolstered by a community of free-thinking women and men.

What I didn't notice was that many of my friends and group members were struggling with the desire to have children and establish families. This emerged at consciousness-raising meetings and, supported by some older women who had become mothers in more traditional marriages, those women who didn't already have kids began to acknowledge their maternal desires and became pregnant. All around me were women giving birth. I would turn up at mother and babies' groups to meet my friends, desperate for serious conversation, only to look around the room and see them (understandably) preoccupied with childcare, talking animatedly to one another about their grisly births, breastfeeding problems, and the horror of sleepless nights. I produced an all-women theatrical event, *Sistershow*, and one night found myself infuriated at those who turned up very late for rehearsal. One woman rebuked and humbled me: 'Before I came out tonight, unlike you, I had to feed and put four children to bed.'

I remember having to suppress my fastidious distaste at going to one woman's flat for a meeting and finding rows of nappies drying all around the room, together with all the other apparatus and smells of a new baby in the bathroom when I went to the loo. I was so glad to return home to my orderly childfree flat; indeed, many of the group who came to my place commented enviously on how neat and tidy it was. I felt smug at that time, relieved I wasn't mired in new motherhood and was able to sleep late at weekends and lock the door behind me, without having to pack the paraphernalia of children for a shopping trip or a walk in the park. I dread to think what my mother-friends felt about me.

For the next thirty years, teaching only adult university students, and engaged in a full-on career in three different cities, I was rarely involved in the daily lives of children, related only half-heartedly to them, and instead pursued a busy adult-oriented life. To tell the truth, this suited me because I found children rather terrifying; their 'otherness' which draws many women to them threw me off course, and I was always at a loss as to how to relate to them. The coolness and hostility mothers sensed me feeling towards their offspring was really an uncomfortable ignorance about how to engage with the very young. This cost me some friendships and meant that I missed developing lifelong relationships with my closest friends' children.

You learn early on that your friends' priorities have changed. Their children will always come first, and even if you aren't exactly an afterthought, that's how you feel. There have been many occasions (often over bank holidays, the long summer months and Christmas) when I've suddenly realised there will be no meetings or phone calls with parent-friends. Family gatherings are sacrosanct and everyone recognises that.

As I got older, I thought I would get my friends back – after the years of preoccupation with their kids, they would be free of family shackles. Selfish, yes, and so short-sighted. For now, many of my friends are in their late sixties or seventies, and they have moved into that special status of grandparent – a lucky position that offers the pleasure of young people with their genes, and the company of offspring for whom they are not ultimately responsible. In a 2021 research study by anthropologist Professor James Rilling, the first to examine grandmothers' brain function, he concludes they 'may be more emotionally connected to their grandkids than to their own sons and daughters'. Why? His argument is: 'Young children have likely evolved traits to be able to manipulate not just the maternal brain, but the grand-maternal brain. An adult child doesn't have the same cute factor, so they may not [receive] the same emotional response.'[7]

Gore Vidal, writing of 'perfect love', advised: 'Never have children, only grandchildren.' From my own experience, this seems very true. Photos of new babies, videos of first steps and laughing toddlers gazing into phone cameras are regularly passed around social gatherings and gym-class groups, to which we are all invited to ooh and aah (and we do). The community of mothers and especially grandmothers is powerful, and all the childless woman can do is admire, congratulate and offer the odd photo of a holiday, garden or dog.

• • •

However, this tale of a simple childless life isn't quite true, and late in my life it had another chapter. Very early one grey Saturday morning in 2006, my partner DJ brought me tea in bed and said he had something to discuss. I waited for him to reveal he had terminal cancer or was going to leave me. In fact, he confessed to me that he had just heard from a lover with whom he'd had a brief summer affair in the iconic year 1968, and from whom he'd never heard since. She had recently found him via the internet, and wanted him to know he had a son, Christoph, born in 1969, a fact she had kept secret for thirty-seven years for the sake of her husband, his adoptive father.

Before DJ and I got together, I had two serious partners who were fathers. One of them, a short relationship of less than two years, gave me my first taste of sharing a man with his children. I discovered he was heavily into drugs and unsure of his own sexuality. His children were very disturbed, and I was horrified to think I would need to take on these poor kids I could barely understand. After many traumatic events, I got out before it was too late. The second partner, Peter, a stable and successful man who separated painfully from his children's mother, became involved with me when they were very young. He was a devoted parent, so losing daily contact with his children was a heavy blow. We had the children to stay at weekends and holidays, making our small study, bedrooms and adult spaces as child-friendly as possible. I was unsettled by the physical presence of two young children – their untidiness, noise, unexpected outbursts of rage and distress – and felt pushed aside by their overwhelming needs. Being a stepmother was never part of my life plan, and I resisted its possible pleasures, instead facing it with a grim conscientiousness and sense of duty to Peter (whom selfishly I wanted all to myself).

Such feelings don't exactly work with children, and – despite everyone's best efforts and some good times – there was many an ugly clash and sulking silence. I particularly remember sitting at the desk in my study while my stepson jabbed bad-temperedly at the wood with a paper knife, asking, 'Why are you always reading a book?' I lived for years with guilt about my incompetence and lack of generosity towards those two lovely young people who never asked for a stepmother. Many years later, at my ex-partner's birthday party, I met his now middle-aged son, who cheered me by saying, 'God, we were horrible to you, Helen.' No more than I deserved, I thought, though in recent years I've read a lot more about the challenges of step-parenting and realise what a tough gig it is. I simply wasn't up to it.

One of the things I most cherished about DJ was the fact he'd never had children, and had enjoyed long relationships with two other women who'd made it clear they didn't want them. A humorous and brilliant man, a great cook and (like me) a homebody, he would have been a fantastic father. However, I told him early in our life together that I wasn't interested in reproducing, and that was never an issue for us – except for a few edgy conversations we had when I had a late period and wondered what to do if I were pregnant.

This latest revelation changed all that. Damn it, my partner – whom I had recently married after twenty-seven years of cohabitation – was, like the others, a father, and also a grandfather of four. I was an instant stepmother and step-grandmother. Still, I was relieved that this was unlikely to affect our daily life together. It was a complicated story. The mother of DJ's son was Italian, married to a German man who raised Christoph as his own. Christoph grew up in Germany but subsequently married a Danish woman, and when we got to know them he had four children aged between two and thirteen, and they were living in an eco-village in Denmark where he'd built his own house and was a central figure in that community. Had they been living in a village outside Bristol, the impact on our lives would have been considerably greater.

Here we go again, I thought. However, being much older and more secure in myself and my relationship than during my time with Peter and his children, I was prepared to give this odd situation a go, especially as DJ was intrigued at the prospect of meeting his son. Even though I felt a pang that this new family had nothing to do with me, I rose to it and argued this could bring a whole new dimension to our childless lives. But there was too much working against us. They lived in another country, involving a difficult and costly journey between our homes. We didn't have a language or culture in common. Christoph and his wife spoke reasonable English and the children were learning at school, but it was hardly an ideal situation to build family bonds across the sea, thirty-seven years late. Nevertheless, in the subsequent years when we visited them, we tried our best. Since no one expects you to learn Danish, DJ learned German but soon realised neither his son nor grandchildren wished to speak that language. However, we had fun teaching the grandchildren words and phrases in English – and Beatles music and lyrics forged a tentative bond between us.

This worked up to a point, while there was early enthusiasm and interest in this new 'family'. The children were intrigued by the strange English speakers who turned up each summer, responding to us with a mixture of curiosity and indifference. We invited the six of them to England, and rented a large house with a spacious garden in the Wye Valley for two weeks, involving a hired bus from Bristol for all of us and my sister-in-law Pauline, and complicated arrangements in a shambolic house. We'd hoped for decent weather: the children gambolling in the garden and wandering along the Wye, with barbecues in the evening and all the doors wide open. Alas, July in Wales did its worst. Every day was cold and windy, and rain poured down spitefully. We hardly ventured into the soggy garden; we took some wet walks through the woods to the river but often half the party turned back; a barbecue was lit one evening during a dry spell, then the heavens opened. We were crammed into the house together with a broken dishwasher and hungry mouths to feed. As the only driver, I spent my time in the car to and from the nearest supermarket, astonished at how much food four children and five adults could get through by the end of breakfast. The child-centredness of my new stepdaughter-in-law made me feel completely irrelevant, while DJ teased me with that Simpsons line: 'Won't somebody please think of the children?'

I recently read Elizabeth Taylor's celebrated 1965 short story, 'The Devastating Boys', featuring a professor's wife, Laura, whose children have left the nest but not yet produced her yearned-for grandchildren, and whose confidence and self-esteem have disappeared in a life as a country-based mother and housewife. Her patronising husband persuades her to offer two 'coloured' children a summer holiday, so – with no support from him – she dutifully welcomes and looks after them for a fortnight, often desperately grasping for activities to try to amuse them. Taylor's unsentimental perspective shows the two boys – with whom Laura rather ineffectually tries to relate – getting along with each other in ways she cannot share or understand. At the end of their visit Laura waves them off at the station (they don't even glance in her direction), and with an aching head and throat 'she had such a sense of failure and fatigue that she hardly knew how to walk back to the car'.[8]

I knew just how Laura felt. But unlike her timid attempts to ingratiate herself with those boys, my response was to avoid intimate contact and get on with practical chores. I hated being cooped up in a house with so many noisy and restless people, having to feed children who all ate different foods (I know this is the experience of many parents, but it was a shock to me). The children were at a Rudolf Steiner school in Denmark's second city, Aarhus, so creativity was central to their lives, but as a bookish swot I couldn't take part in all the drawing and craft-making their mother and my early-years-expert sister-in-law initiated. Apart from driving and shopping, I felt utterly superfluous; I was shy of these strange foreign kids and their parents, and couldn't relate to them spontaneously or joyfully. I just felt pissed off – and one day when we were visiting a steam-train station, I walked away along the road for about two miles shouting into the air and wishing terrible harm on everyone around me. Why was I suddenly being forced into a role I'd never wanted with people I hardly knew?

As I write these words, I hate myself for that lack of openness and empathy towards stepchildren, and I marvel at those women who can treat them as their own. What startled me most was the way all our friends were thrilled at this sudden family discovery (one male friend even wept with joy) and were seeing us in a very different light. I was uncomfortably aware that they must always have felt we were rather sad and lacking fulfilment, while now we were wholly part of the human race. How could they know how little delight this instant family had brought me, and that it just underlined my own sense of helplessness around the young and my failure to enter into a new sort of family life?

We have all met several times since, though communication has been sparse. And things have changed for the better. In 2024, Christoph and one of his sons, nineteen-year-old Cornelius, came to visit us for a few days in Bristol. They were charming and witty, with impeccable English (putting native English speakers to shame), and cheerfully participated in our daily life, helping with gardening and small jobs round the house. Selfishly, I was reminded of how delightful it is to have a young person with a lifetime's computer knowledge to resolve your mobile and software problems. And it gave me insight into the joy and stimulation, not to mention the intergenerational perspectives, that can be gained from having younger people in your life. In a delightful postscript to this, our grandson met our great-nephew in Bristol and they went sailing together round the Danish coast. For a while, I felt part of an intergenerational family group.

Who are 'Our' Children and Grandchildren?

In my preface, I mentioned Duncan Macmillan's prescient play *Lungs*, about a young couple's debates over whether to have a child. A provocative question gets thrown out: 'The icecaps are melting, there's overpopulation, political unrest; everything's going to hell in a handcart – why on earth would someone bring a baby into this world?' Eight years later, in the *Observer*, questions were posed to teenage climate activist Greta Thunberg. One was: 'I am an old man without children. Why should I care about what happens to the planet after my death?' Greta's response was: 'Maybe you believe in something? Like karma, faith? Or morality? Or just because it's the right thing to do.'[1] She herself has not ruled out having children in future.

All my adult life, I've listened to the solemn pronouncements of politicians and pundits about what we are creating for and leaving to 'our children and grandchildren'. This is designed to add weight and solemnity to social and political changes, and to ensure the speaker or pundit seems responsible and caring.

If someone is talking about new social policies, the claim that they will enhance future generations seems to prove their seriousness and makes it clear this isn't just about 'me' or my political ambitions. Nowhere is this more noticeable than in debates about climate change. What is the responsibility of older generations to the young and as-yet unborn? Perhaps because we cannot face imagining a final apocalypse when we all drown or are swept away by monstrous fires or ice storms, nuclear war or AI technology, we tend to domesticate the arguments and focus them on individuals, including our own families. When Prince Harry and Meghan Markle announced they would have a maximum of two children so as to reduce their impact on the earth – something for which the charity Population Matters later gave them a sustainability award – this was read by some as a rebuke to Prince William for already having three. But it was also a heads-up to couples discussing their carbon footprint.

Although this rhetoric of 'our' children and grandchildren has become very clichéd, it remains powerful, and underlines the centrality of family relationships in our society. If I see that something will have an effect on 'my' son or daughter, and 'their/our' children, I can endorse it and argue apparently selflessly for it. But there is often a very selfish motive, focused on 'my' family. The number of times you see politicians and media figures refer back to their own offspring is a reminder of the way we often think too narrowly and perhaps narcissistically about future generations. These statements always make me feel like the child in the room.

Writer Geoff Dyer provocatively suggests, 'Parenthood, far from enlarging one's worldview, results in an appalling form of myopia. Hence André Gide's verdict on families, "those misers of love".[2] There are ungenerous judgements of this kind in both camps. In 2016, Andrea Leadsom MP, a candidate for the Conservative Party leadership, cast doubt on Theresa May's aspiration to become prime minister because she wasn't a mother, forcing out of May the sad admission that she and her husband had 'failed' to produce offspring. Cruel though it was, it pinpointed a widespread view that anyone without children probably hasn't the right to talk of future generations because they're not personally invested. Theresa May might try to imagine the families of the future, but she didn't have the personal experience and knowledge that parenting gives, and thus the compassion and empathy to make vital decisions about the people she would lead. That same year, Turkish president Recep Tayyip Erdoğan claimed women without children were deficient and incomplete, and giving up on humanity.

On 31 July 2021, journalist Arwa Mahdawi reported that the US Ohio Republican Senate candidate made a speech chastising four prominent Democrat leaders – Vice President Kamala Harris and three others – for not reproducing, suggesting that not having kids made them bad leaders with no 'physical commitment to the future' of the US.[3] Right-wing Fox News then seriously debated whether the 'childless left' deserves a vote. In 2024, Republican vice presidential candidate J. D. Vance repeated the charge, this time against Democrat presidential candidate Kamala Harris, that as one of a group of 'childless cat ladies who are miserable at their own lives' she had 'no direct stake' in America. Among others, reluctantly childless actor Jennifer Aniston spoke out, charging Vance with being against expanding IVF treatment that would enable more women to become mothers.

Of course, this is dangerous rhetoric. But as someone who chose not to have children, I feel there is a tad of truth that parents bind communities together. It is something we should be careful about as more and more women delay or decide against childbearing.

The Ties That Bind

Think about it. You get pregnant and are immediately involved in a medical system, in most cases the NHS, with hospital visits, midwives or health workers, childbirth classes, and mother and baby groups. Despite the deficiencies in health services (which have increased dramatically in recent years), these will lock you into a network of caring organisations and groups of other parents that will see you through the next decades as your child(ren) grows up. You then engage with schools of various kinds: nurseries, playgroups, primary schools and so on. The school run and school gates are a major part of your life, and a gregarious as well as competitive meeting place for others in your situation.

You will attend your GP surgery and probably your local hospital on many occasions, for antenatal and postnatal care, inoculations, kids' minor or major illnesses; and you'll visit local shops, libraries, day-care centres, coffee shops and neighbours' homes for necessary purchases, reading matter, advice and help with your children. Many of the women and men you meet there may become lifelong friends. Health will become a key concern as your offspring catch the usual diseases or are diagnosed with autism, diabetes, epilepsy, long Covid. As your children grow older, the secondary-school system demands you engage with their syllabus and career choices, as well as attending parents' evenings and school plays. You will be drawn into your contemporaries' debates about the age at which children should receive mobile phones and gain access to social media. If your kids are lucky and talented enough, they'll go into apprenticeship, training or further and higher education, and you will support them through the exam system, helping them make major decisions about their future, visiting workplaces, college open days and so forth. If you are a single and/or LGBTQ+ parent, these networks are important in cementing connections with others and avoiding isolation or discrimination.

When/if your children have their own children, the whole process is in some ways replicated. Increasingly, as women need or choose to work outside the home, and with childcare prohibitively expensive, grandparents – if based locally or willing to travel – take up the job of unpaid childminders and carers, taking kids to nursery, school, the GP, museums and libraries. The support and love of grandparents can be seen in the large numbers of strollers pushed by older people (usually women) occupying the streets during working hours. If parents are lucky, grandparents will help with not only regular childcare but also finances, family holidays and luxuries. Those bonds between children and their grandparents can be an important intergenerational buffer between parents and kids, and lead to special lifelong relationships.

These connections and relationships are what constitute 'society' and 'community', and they are the ties that bind – the props and networks that get people through and bring them closely together. Next time you are at your hairdresser's, in any social situation with your peers, watching TV or listening to radio programmes, note how often women share thoughts about or indirectly reference their children and grandchildren, often illustrated with phone photos. The rapid development of Facebook and WhatsApp family groups, Zoom meetings, email, Instagram and SMS – among all social classes, genders and ethnic groups – strengthens those connections and enables informal daily catch-ups. However fraught relations are within families and between parents and children, this connectedness on a daily or regular basis digs deep roots into a collective empathetic humanity.

Several of my friends – not to mention female journalists – are cynical about this collective spirit, especially when they are the carers of elderly, sick parents who take up huge amounts of their energy at a point when they yearn for space and time. But in *An Extra Pair of Hands: A Story of Caring, Ageing and Everyday Acts of Love* (2021), the moving account of caring for her aged parents and mother-in-law, Kate Mosse emphasises the loving bonds between different generations which – whatever the practical and emotional challenges – enrich the lives of and communication between grandparents, parents and children.[4] In Chimamanda Ngozi Adichie's paean to her dead father, *Notes on Grief* (2021), the writer's magnificent tribute to a beloved parent reminds us that family is at the centre of all societies and still offers the profoundest relationships and most emotional satisfaction of our lives.[5]

If you have no children, and are not a carer, little of this applies. Yes, you may have nieces and nephews with whom you are close; you may have friends' children who feel like your own; you may run a Scout, Guide or church group, or volunteer to play games and teach skills to children. But if you're not a biological, adoptive or foster parent, you will be outside (or can opt out of) most of those networks that are at the heart of our family-oriented society. You don't need to engage with the politics and daily problems of childcare facilities and organisation; you don't need to know what Key Stages 1, 2 and 3 are, and how difficult it is to get your precious ones, with their siblings, into the school of choice. You don't have to attend to their mental or physical health, food preferences and fads, and deal with playground and social media bullying. You won't live with that dull throb of anxiety most parents feel constantly about what might happen to their child.

This doesn't mean you don't engage with many of those issues. Good citizens will want to see (and lobby for) affordable nurseries, small class sizes, fewer tests for very young children, and opportunities in further and higher education for all young people. Many people without children are school governors, local councillors, magistrates, and arts and sports board members.

You care about your nephews and nieces and your friends' and neighbours' children, and you offer support to their parents through the many joys and agonies of their growing up. But you probably don't feel any of this on the pulses in the visceral way that parents do, and – as I hear many a grandparent say – you can always turn your back or hand them back. You also won't ever feel the utter agony of losing a child, as a few of my friends have done. There is probably no way you can really understand such grief – except vicariously through listening to personal accounts and consuming fiction, memoir, or film and TV treatments. I have sat listening to women describing their losses of children from illness, accident or suicide, but I've always known nothing that has happened to me – losing both parents, cousins, very close friends – could ever measure up to this.

In September 2021, I listened to the heartbroken mother of Sarah Everard, raped and murdered brutally by a policeman. When Susan Everard described never again being able to hold her daughter, but instead hugging her dressing gown that still smells of her, I heard anguish and despair deeper than anything I had ever known. In recent years, the agony of parents and families in war zones within Ukraine and Gaza has been heartbreaking, though outside my own lived experience.

The Coronavirus Crisis

So the family takes centre stage in our society, and – as Shakespeare and other great writers have shown us – the dramas, tragedies and triumphs of life are usually experienced within the family, with the single and childless/free sidelined and silenced. Images of war- or famine-torn countries where mothers cling to starving babies, walk miles to get water for their children, and scream with heartbreak as their families are separated or killed, are a constant reminder of the most important relationship human beings can have. In the UK, nowhere was this more clearly articulated than in the events following the 2020 outbreak of Coronavirus, with a series of lockdowns and a huge shift in social intercourse. Households were restricted so that extended families were unable to mingle, and children, parents and grandparents were forcibly separated for long periods of time, with serious illness and many deaths experienced in isolation.

Technology was the only thing making 'family' separation bearable. Phone calls, Zoom, social media – for those who had access – brought families and friends together, in some ways more intensely than before, when busy lives had prevented it. The physical interactivity of families was long gone, so increasingly 'family' was almost TV or radio programmes, realised only on screens or via FaceTime calls. My niece took food to her father – my brother, then in his late seventies – and sat in his garden while he talked to her on his phone from the conservatory. My friend Sue drove to her granddaughter's home with a sewing machine, left it on the doorstep, and then through Zoom showed the teenager how to sew face masks for the family.

The weekly doorstep clapping for essential services, especially the NHS, allowed families to emerge from front doors to celebrate the notion of community. The slogan at the time was 'all in this together' – something that failed to recognise the very real class and ethnic differences in our experiences of lockdown. Such communality seemed fragile indeed as evidence of Prime Minister Boris Johnson's rule-breaking 'Partygate' government emerged, and the same government then failed to reward health workers financially. Hopeful rainbows painted by children and 'Bear Hunt' teddy bears, referencing Michael Rosen's famous kids' story, *We're Going on a Bear Hunt*, appeared in people's windows. Meanwhile, statistics of domestic abuse rose to new levels. Being locked down at home with a violent partner heralded a whole new threat to family life. One night, my neighbour had a knock on her door from a terrified woman afraid for her life; the police and ambulance arrived quickly to treat her. But where did she go, and were her children safe?

And, bizarrely, we were *all* 'family'. In the first two weeks after Boris Johnson told us to stay at home to save the NHS and lives, I received a large number of emails from the usual commercial suspects who post daily – Marks & Spencer, Asda, Inn Travel, Bloom & Wild, John Lewis – reiterating that slogan, 'we are all in this together'. Anabel and Barnabas from Neal's Yard Remedies sent me a message 'from our family to yours'; the White Company's CEO, Chrissie, included me in her family and urged 'let's keep chatting. Be kind, be strong, stick together, take care.' Watershed in Bristol assured me that, although their building was shut for now, 'our arms are wide open'. For me, this all became too cloying by far. I was staying at home with DJ, and although sharing the collective vibe at a distance, I didn't need to feel part of any commercial 'family'.

On 30 April 2020, in the midst of the first Coronavirus lockdown, writer Damien Barr tweeted, 'The news is full of talk of families and realising what and who is important in the context of Corona. Then they show pictures of cute kids. Just going to say this again: Not all families have children. You do not need children to be part of a family.' I've certainly had many a conversation with gay and lesbian friends about what a 'family' consists of, and of course many people who don't identify as heteronormative are always facing identity and self-definition challenges outside those norms. In this century, the growing emphasis within the media and literature on the importance and variety of non-sexual friendships has come from young singletons and LBGTQ+ groups resisting the nuclear family. Barr's words were a good corrective to the dominant narrative of family being biological.

Childless at Christmas

But however much you resist that narrative, there's one time of year when you can't escape its full force – and when our feelings about 'family' are tested to the limit: Christmas. Whether or not you have children, whether your own religion allows you to celebrate or avoid a Christian festival, this long holiday period is a testing time for reflecting on the family you have or lack, the fractured relationships you regret, and the arrangements you need to make to rise to this special time. As I know from my early experiences of stepmotherhood, it's often a tense time when children spend this special occasion with one parent, while the other feels their absence and has to make the most of FaceTime calls and WhatsApp. The first Christmas I spent with a partner and his children, in pre-mobile phone or social media days, his ex-wife rang the children every couple of hours – an upsetting experience for us all. Christmas is notoriously a time when many couples decide to split up. The rhetoric of the whole season is especially hard for single parents, singletons, divorced people and blended families. A friend wrote to tell me she'd overheard a friend's husband asking his wife who was going to have the 'waifs and strays' (his single brother and niece) for Christmas Day; this hurt terribly because – as neither a wife nor mother – my friend felt devalued.

In 2019, the last full Christmas before Covid changed everything, I found myself thinking hard about this. Despite my best attempts to ignore it all, the relentless media glorification of families – from the Holy Family itself to those supposed to gather together during this festive season – gets to me. When a churchgoing child, I loved the sense of anticipation, from Advent through to Christmas Day, and the excitement of the birth of Christ the Lord. I wept through many a moving performance of Handel's *Messiah*. As I lost faith, and no longer attended Christmas services, that joy gave way to a general irritation with all the season had come to mean: the consumerism; the race around the shops to stock up on special food; the exhaustion and frustration of travel to be with members of your closest family, leaving your friends behind. For many people of non-Christian faiths, the whole business must be either tedious or intolerable.

Almost all of our siblings, nephews and nieces live a long way from us, and none of us meets up at Christmas as travel and accommodation are just too difficult. My niece asked one year whether we had a Christmas tree, and I felt a miserabilist in telling her we hadn't bothered. We had in previous years, usually when cooking for friends on Christmas Day, but that year – inviting only people who were estranged from their children or partners – we just bought some flowers and dried twigs and a string of upmarket gold-leaf lights ordered from posh gardener Sarah Raven. By the sixth or seventh day of Christmas, as ever, I was sick to death of family films, a Queen's Speech proclaiming her own family joys (and keeping very quiet about their multiple problems and feuds), and adverts of children tearing open packages with starry eyes, while parents sat in a large crowd round a groaning board, which appeared magically without involving anyone's labour. I found myself recalling a wonderful Christmas that DJ and I had spent alone in Exeter, where I was then working. On Christmas Day, we'd made some turkey sandwiches, driven to the seaside resort Budleigh Salterton, and walked along the Otter River in bright if cold sunshine, stopping only to have a little picnic with wine and chocolate. While sitting on the riverbank, we saw a kingfisher, and life felt good.

I was cheered to find echoes of my own lack of enthusiasm about a family Christmas in the words of writer Rose Macaulay, who never married or gave birth (though she had a long-term lover), and wrote articles and novels wittily critical of the norms of femininity and domesticity. In December 1917, at a time when many women were awaiting the return of husbands and sons from the Great War, she and other authors and celebrities were asked to contribute to a feature in the magazine, *The Quiver*, about what they considered the ideal Christmas. While the majority favoured a Christian and/or war theme, or a Dickensian time of food, fun and family togetherness, Macaulay's contribution was to describe a fantasy of being in a country at summertime, such as New Zealand, in a villa full of fruit trees by the sea:

> I should spend the day largely in bathing and cruising in my canoe about the islands off the coast. I should be so far from England that no-one in it could expect me to send them cards or to write, though my friends would, out of kindness to my loneliness, write to me. It would therefore be a Christmas spent in receiving without giving – an ideal state. There would be no war going on – or, if there were, I should be too far from it to hear about it. Peace, warmth, the sea, and no obligations – nothing else is, I think, necessary.[6]

When I first read that, I thought that echoed my own desire for a simple, decommercialised non-family Christmas.

However, during that same Christmas period, I watched a BBC Four documentary about singer Janet Baker, who retired at forty-eight and in her eighties was caring for her husband who'd had a stroke – and who loved (as she did not) to listen to her music. She had decided against having children, presumably for professional reasons, and I tried to resist feeling there was something sad about the two of them holding hands in their sitting room, with a paid carer who was possibly a surrogate son. I reflected on the fact that even those with great careers can end up in isolation and sorrow. I wondered whether she'd regretted abandoning her professional life in middle age, and I feared that I too might end up in that tableau, wishing I was surrounded by a noisy and caring multigenerational family.

The following year, 2020, Prime Minister Boris Johnson 'cancelled' Christmas because of the prevalence of the Delta variant of Covid, and it was well-nigh impossible for families to gather together to celebrate. So the resumption of a festive season (at least in England) in 2021 led to elaborate travel arrangements, large family gatherings and parties. DJ and I rose to the occasion with a dinner for the family of our niece and nephew, Kate and Ceri, lunch for my older brother Geoffrey and partner Valerie, and invitations to friends and neighbours for drinks and nibbles. Our friends, who lavished invitations, visits and phone calls on us, were obviously a little concerned we were having Christmas Day alone: sleeping late, reading in bed, walking, eating and drinking, binge-watching TV . . . such hardship! As we indulged ourselves, in a modest reminder of familial links we received a one-line email of seasonal good wishes from DJ's son, Christoph.

Out of the Loop

If you have no children, you are marginalised in the whole merry-go-round of family responsibilities, obligations and pleasures. As a result, your thoughts about parent-child relationships inevitably draw you back into your own position as child. Memories – whether happy or sad– are tinged by the power struggle between you and your mother and/or father, and your feelings about parents are always about those who parented you, not you as parent. This means you remain – at some level – infantilised, irresponsible or curiously dependent. Many childfree women have echoed my own feeling that they're not really grown-up.

When our parents die, and we become orphans, the generational vacuum can seem overwhelming. I have no one to parent me, and no one to parent. The powerful mother's voice in my head is now imaginary, and the approval or disapproval of the mother is gone. I know that I am not the first woman to look in the mirror the day after her mother's death and see her mother's face in her own. She had returned, incorporated into my body and soul, and I was both child and mother. I felt horribly alone and yet also liberated – though in subsequent years I've realised how the tension between those emotions remains and even grows. The strongest feeling I have retained to this day is a profound regret I didn't ask my mother more penetrating questions about her life and her attitude towards her own family and the family she created with my father. I know this is a common regret, and I always urge friends to try to engage their parents in such conversations before it's too late.

As it is for all other animal species, the weighty task of bringing new life into the world and nurturing it through to independence is the most important anyone takes on – and the childless are out of the adult part of that loop. It's interesting to read of writers such as Kenneth Grahame and Virginia and Leonard Woolf using babyish language or fanciful names with their partners. Olivia Laing describes its prevalence in Grahame's courtship of his future wife Elspeth: 'Marriage proposals, wedding plans and negotiations around living arrangements were all carried out in this nursery prattle, which allowed both participants to play at being children adrift in a mystifyingly adult world.' Discussing the forty-three-year marriage between Iris Murdoch and John Bayley, Laing relates that Bayley described 'the world they inhabited as a sort of kingdom of childhood, in which they communicated via a private babble quite separate from the professorial fluidities they employed elsewhere'. She quotes Martin Amis's suggestion that the couple 'suffered collectively from *nostalgie de la boue,* literally the desire to return to the sticky mud of one's origins, the ooze and squalor of infancy'.[7] And while I know *families* use secret or special linguistic codes and vocabulary, beginning with those semi-incoherent communications with tiny babies and family pets, there are many childless couples who employ a 'private babble' they share with no one else. DJ and I have a playful conversational mode that would be incomprehensible to others.

When critics describe the childless as irresponsible, unnatural, and unable to speak for future generations, they mean that we have opted out of life's biggest challenge because we are regressing from adult life and duties. However, that the childless are the only ones wishing to escape from adulthood's burdens and revert to infancy's 'ooze and squalor', I very much doubt.

Chapter 3

How to find Meaning and Legacy in a Childfree Life

When she was forty-seven and beyond childbearing age, the writer Jody Day founded Gateway Women, with its tagline 'United by and Beyond Childlessness' and its aim to provide a 'global friendship and support network for childless women'. She has gained many followers, initially from a blog, then through her 2013 book, *Living the Life Unexpected: How to Find Hope, Meaning and A Fulfilling Future Without Children*. She reassures women: 'You are not a failure. You haven't screwed up. You are not alone.'[1] Referred to as the 'Grand Dame of Childlessness' and 'the Beyoncé of Childlessness', in a keynote lecture she reminded her audience that one in five women born in the 1960s are childless – 80 per cent by circumstance ('social infertility'), 10 per cent by medical circumstance, and 10 per cent by choice.[2]

Having been childless and heartbroken with 'babymania' in her post-divorce early forties, Day argues that a childless woman is grieving her identity *over the life course*: grand-motherhood, great grand-motherhood, being a "soccer mom"... the children's

49

birthday parties, teaching them to ride a bike, visiting them when they leave college or the graduation ceremonies . . .' Her books, courses and workshops are designed to help women through their sense of loss and failure in a 'pronatalist' society. Claiming that our culture has lost the sense of 'elders', and there is no word for older women other than 'grandmother', she accepts the notion of witches, and wants them to inspire her.[3]

There is a plethora of labels for women without children. Jody Day cites terms denoting the way childless women are outsiders in mainstream culture: apart from the obvious 'childless' and 'childfree', she includes 'DINK' (double income, no kids), 'PANK' (professional aunt, no kids), 'GINK' (green inclinations, no kids) and her own term 'NoMo' (an abbreviation of 'not- or non-mother'). She also lists the words women on her courses and at her workshops have come up with for older childless women: 'spinster, old maid, crazy old cat lady, career woman, dried-up old bag, bat or hag, maiden aunt, wicked or evil stepmother, witch'. I admire Day's spirited discovery of 'the hidden power within childless women stereotypes'. Some examples of her reworkings: 'spinster, old maid', which is normally defined as 'an unpartnered mature childless woman', becomes 'independent, competent, confident, creative, resourceful, educated, financially independent, free, liberated and worldly-wise. Powerful.' And 'witch' – 'an outspoken childless older woman' – is for Day 'confident, courageous, fierce, knowledgeable, self-aware and unapologetic. Powerful.' To her, these various negative archetypes reveal 'the suppression of feminine power'.[4] As a counter-narrative to our pronatalist society, Day's brave words provide inspirational support to women who feel they have failed.

Like many less sophisticated self-help books, Day's focuses on her own involuntary childlessness and tracks a fifteen-year 'journey' to a better psychological and emotional place. She acknowledges that she is still recovering, and the gap in her life will never fully close, but she offers her readers the hope they can find a new way of living without motherhood. What is startling about her account is the fact that so many women have never been able to speak to family or friends about their sorrow and the many trials through which they have gone in order to conceive or adopt. This is another 'problem with no name', and here Day uncovers a reservoir of misery, hopelessness and lost dreams. The pejorative terms relating to childlessness were greeted with a furore during the 2024 US presidential election race when Donald Trump, his 'First Buddy' Elon Musk and vice presidential candidate Vance – all flaunting large numbers of their own children (and in Musk's case offering to impregnate the childfree star Taylor Swift) – made it clear they felt childless women had no direct stake in the country's future. Jody Day's writing and group work have helped to counter that crude anti-feminist rhetoric.

Though voluntarily childless/free, I too have rarely discussed the matter with other people. Friends and acquaintances who have no children . . . well, I used to assume insensitively they didn't want them – unless they suddenly exploded with sorrow or anger and told me their stories. I recall a lunchtime conversation with a former colleague and friend where I casually said that I didn't think women, or indeed men, 'have the right' to have a child. The fury in her eyes as she said how wrong I was, and how it was every woman's right to give birth, hinted at a whole personal history I'd never guessed, and also demonstrated to me that my view was highly controversial. Our friendship never recovered.

In talking to friends about this subject, I learned that few had been asked why they didn't have children, or what they thought about the subject. Other women, however, said that, when asked, they resort to a variety of replies. A teacher told me she responds by saying she works all day with children and doesn't have energy for any more (or she turns the tables and asks why the questioner has children); another woman said she holds back from saying 'because having children seemed a selfish act'. One woman related that when she was younger she'd say she didn't want them, and the response was invariably 'You'll change your mind when you get older.' Another mentioned that her reply, 'My husband and I are infertile,' was a conversation stopper. A well-travelled professional woman recalled being in a taxi in Uganda and being questioned by the driver if she had children. When she said no, he said, 'Is a life worth living without having children?' She turned the tables, challenging him to say why he'd asked her this, and she dared him to say he had never known a woman without children who had done extraordinary things or explored other pathways than childbirth. She said that, after she left the taxi, he seemed very thoughtful.

If you're prominent in the media or public life, everyone feels they have a right to comment on this most private of choices or situations. Former politicians Nicola Sturgeon and Julia Gillard are seen as suspect, and film stars Helen Mirren and Jennifer Aniston are constantly scrutinised for their childless status. Despite her constant reiteration of no regrets, Mirren's comment that she sobbed for twenty minutes after seeing the 1989 film *Parenthood* was seized on as evidence that she was in denial. A description of Aniston's 'unused womb' led her to publish a detailed statement in the *Huffington Post* in which she criticised the tabloids' 'perpetuation of the notion that women are somehow incomplete, unsuccessful or unhappy if they're not married with children'. Novelist Ann Patchett told BBC Radio 4 *Woman's Hour* that she'd been asked repeatedly to write about her childless state, and had only done so when there was a gap in her new essay collection. Once she started to write, 'Flames were shooting out of my fingers,' she said, concluding: 'It's a choice.'[5]

The late writer Hilary Mantel claimed that journalists and critics were sometimes coercive in trying to make a story out of her childlessness – which was caused by what she saw as the most significant shaper of her life, endometriosis. That terrible disease, in her case self-diagnosed and confirmed far too late, led to treatments which skewed her metabolism so she put on a large amount of weight. For years people would ask her the dreaded question, 'When is it due?' And Mantel told me that when BBC Two's *The Culture Show* visited to film her for a feature: 'They suggested that we go to a nearby children's playground, and that I sit on a bench and watch the children and look upset, and they film me. I said no, of course. But isn't that almost laughably monstrous?'[6] It seems that, the more distinguished or famous you are, the more you invite critical scrutiny about your childlessness.

Young and Childfree

The media – and social media – are full of descriptions by women aged between twenty and forty on their ambivalent feelings about having children. There are women anguishing over their miscarriages, stillbirths, inability to get pregnant, and the difficulty of IVF, but there are also many who are having conversations with themselves and others about the desirability of bringing new life into the world, and the associated costs to a woman's life, relationships, financial position and career. Author of a book about her own childlessness, *Self-Contained: Scenes from a Single Life* (2021), journalist Emma John reports that there are a fast-growing number of women who have never married and who live alone (between 2002 and 2018, the number doubled). While China talks of 'Leftover Women', in South Korea the 'old miss' in her forties has been transformed into the single-and-affluent 'gold miss'.[7]

Echoing Jody Day, John looks back over the reputation and representation of 'the spinster' since the Middle Ages: from the outsider figure defined and punished as a 'witch' to the respectable spinster of thread and yarn who could support herself and maintain financial independence, and then the nineteenth-century spinster joining the first female professions – governess and nurse, expanding to typing, journalism, academia and law. Many of these women became philanthropists and agitators, educators and explorers. In the twenty-first century, the spinster is either enviably or pitiably childfree – a career woman or a failed mother. In Madeline Miller's novel *Circe*, the protagonist's brother Aeëtes – talking of Scylla, whom Circe has made monstrous – describes an ugly nymph as 'nothing, less than nothing' who will never marry or have children and so will be 'a burden to her family, a stain upon the face of the world ... scorned and reviled'. However, he says, a monster 'always has a place. She may have all the glory her teeth can snatch. She will not be loved for it, but she will not be constrained either.'[8]

Emma John herself enthuses about the contemporary 'single-positivity movement', though she concedes that her sister's announcement she was to be a mother meant 'becoming an aunt', which 'brought with it a phantom modifier, one that echoed across my empty flat, even though no one had spoken it aloud'. She blames her reading history – finding that spinsters in Austen, Dickens and P. G. Wodehouse were 'figures of fun and frustration' with 'petty vendettas and outsize jealousies'. Like many childless professional women, John is aware that she can be seen as a failure, despite the 'empty flat' she is lucky enough to occupy. And although she doesn't plan it right now, with the increasing popularity among her generation of freezing eggs for future conception, engaging surrogate mothers and adopting from overseas, she will have plenty of time to consider making that empty flat a baby's home.[9] She might also look to the example of Julia Peyton-Jones, retired director of the Serpentine Gallery, who at sixty-four brought home a baby girl from California and justified this on the grounds that – if she were to die before her daughter, Pia, had grown up – the girl's care would immediately be taken over by Julia's five sisters, many nephews and nieces, and thirty-seven (yes!) godparents, including several distinguished art historians.

When I was in my twenties and thirties, egg freezing, surrogacy and international adoption weren't at the centre of popular discourse. These were the decades when you had to make up your mind, because after forty and especially menopause (which in some women could come 'too early'), your choice was made for you. Lesbian women could use DIY kits to inseminate, but most people conceived in the old-fashioned way. I well remember hearing my friends debating their options, and sharing the reasons they wanted to be mothers: satisfying a deep primal urge to give birth; having someone to care for; cementing a partnership/marriage; continuing a family heritage; having someone to look after them in old age. My response to all these now seems rather simplistic. I had never felt a biological urge, and I knew there was evidence that children were as likely to break up a marriage as to hold it together. I didn't care about my family continuing beyond my death, and I was pretty sure any children wouldn't be around to care for me during old-age infirmity. But I look around now and see that many people, including my friends and work colleagues, got what they wanted. They have grown-up children who are living interesting (albeit often complex) lives, caring for their own children but also spending leisure time and regular holidays with their parents, and certainly attending to them as they become frail or ill. Even when children live on different continents or are unable to visit ageing parents, bonding and familial continuity are kept alive via Facebook, FaceTime and Zoom.

And this isn't just a white middle-class phenomenon. In all communities – especially in the midst of a cost-of-living crisis and amid cultural and social deprivation, leading many adults to remain living with parents as they are unable to afford their own homes – the family is having to serve as a major social service. This doesn't mean it is all sweetness and light. I'm not naive enough to believe these relationships work smoothly. Families are challenged at all times and can be dysfunctional, while children and parents can have antagonistic relationships for many reasons, with homelessness sometimes the disastrous result. Writers have often explored such broken ties or family resentments. Feminist authors such as Rachel Cusk, Julie Myerson and Lily Dunn have written frankly and often bitterly about parental relationships with children, and I'm well aware of the frictions, disappointments and mutual antagonism that exist at all stages of life among even the happiest of families. How wrong Tolstoy was to say all happy families are alike. There is no formula for happiness, and in order to function, all families must adjust, compromise, forgive and forget.

As a teenager, I wanted to get away from my parents as soon as possible, in order to live a personal, sexual and political life of which I knew they would disapprove. I look back now and see how hurt they must have been that I visited rarely and kept so much of my life from them – though it was hard to go home and have bitter political arguments, especially around the socialist feminism to which I was deeply committed. I didn't realise, all those years ago, that a busy work life is no permanent substitute for family or community, especially as it winds down into retirement. I thought of myself as a 'career woman' and – despite having a happy home life – committed most of my time to teaching, students, colleagues and publications. Because of the way universities evaluate academics, I spent many a dreary hour doing repetitive administration, completing forms asking me how many articles and books I'd written, how many courses devised and taught, how many external examinerships accepted, PhD theses examined, etc., etc. I was rewarded for my diligence with small bonuses, invitations onto national committees, and promotions to higher grades. In so many ways, academics are needy, swotty children who've never really left school because they always yearn for gold stars.

Older and Childfree

I fear this is true of me – the insecure schoolgirl still seeking adult approval. For decades, the top-of-the-class gold-star culture satisfied my desire for recognition, and my colleagues made me feel part of a privileged if horribly competitive world in which we all strove to excel and – if lucky – watched one another's backs. I was uncomfortably aware that I appeared to have more in common with the majority of my male colleagues than some of the women with whom I worked. I never took time out for maternity leave; I could make breakfast meetings without having to do the school run; I worked late in the office not needing to rush back to put children to bed, sort clothes, make packed lunches and prepare school bags; my conversations were largely about work and rarely about my home life. Even if that life was of supreme importance to me, working always among more male than female colleagues I often felt like a token man, a less-than-woman in a patriarchal world. For five years, as the only female head of a large department (out of twenty or so), I tried to speak for and represent women's issues and female colleagues' problems at the most senior level, but was aware of how suspicious men were about any hint of feminist arguments or talk of domestic issues. We didn't discuss the menopause, recipes or bad-hair days, and they rarely mentioned those children whose photos were sitting proudly on their desks. I resented the patronising tone many senior men took towards women workers who put their families first, especially secretarial, administrative and cleaning staff with whom I easily developed a female bond. My last years as a senior academic reminded me of the contradictory roles I'd always played as a childfree woman: one of the boys, but also down among the women.

In my final working decade, I stopped teaching to take on a part-time role developing an arts and culture strategy for the university – working alone and no longer part of an academic department. Only then did I realise how tentative those work-based collegial ties were, and it hit me that retirement would mean losing the casual but friendly communications that ensured I felt part of a lively, active and – most of all – *young* community. I had always scorned those colleagues who came back to the department after retiring, popping into offices to see people, chatting to the secretaries, seeking the gossip. So

I avoided that, and when I left my final post, I didn't look back and rarely returned in person. It helped that I lived in a different city and had book contracts, but it meant that, overnight, I fell out of touch with younger people. Much of the satisfaction, and perhaps significance, of my entire career was gone.

I reflected on this when I read about the death of one of my former colleagues. Like me, a childless woman (though, unlike me, single), she had been an eccentric professor, and when I was her boss I'd had to cope with her strange demands and the fact she'd changed her office door lock so the cleaners – about whom she was paranoid – could no longer enter. I'd forgotten about her, but then in 2016 a name caught my eye when there was a scandal about her death by suicide. Police had smashed her front door to remove from her the euthanasia pills she'd ordered illegally online from Exit International. This upset her arrangements (including having written to family and friends, alerting them to her plans), but a week later – using some other pills secreted in her house – she ended her life, just not in the meticulous way she'd planned. When journalist Katie Engelhart had interviewed her some months before this, she'd found a rational woman who had multiple health problems and was tired of living an uncomfortable and painful life. 'People with a terminal illness are the lucky ones,' Avril said. 'I have longed for a diagnosis of cancer.' She told Engelhart that if her father had still been alive, she would not be killing herself. But he was long dead. So were her mother, aunts and uncles, and her two cats. There were still a few cousins around, and their families.

'I love them all, but that doesn't in any way affect my decision,' she said. 'They are not that relevant in my life.'[10]

I was shaken by this story, since I too have long supported the idea of voluntary euthanasia and hope to die peacefully without intrusive interventions. As Avril did, I have cousins, nieces and nephews whom I see rarely, and apart from my two dear brothers (who live a distance away and may not outlive me), those relatives still around won't be too affected by my death, fond as I hope they are of me. I no longer have any parents or cats, and no great desire to live to a great age – especially if incapacitated. My partner is older than me, so we both anticipate (possibly wrongly) that I will outlive him. Would I be more eager to live a long life and to accept medical interventions if I had biological children and indeed grandchildren? I rather think I would.

There's a new narrative developing about old age. In an attempt to stifle longstanding prejudices about and discrimination towards the elderly, commentators are celebrating the advantages of age, and the many ways active old people can ensure a long and healthy life. We're reminded that retired people sit on boards, volunteer in charity shops, do childcare for their grandkids, join U3A (University of the Third Age) groups, play tennis and bowls. They get new knees and hips, go line-dancing, and relish the sex they can have with partners without guilt or fear of pregnancy. What is suppressed in these stories are the many humiliations and sufferings of the creaking ageing body – Shakespeare's 'second childishness and mere oblivion; Sans teeth, sans eyes, sans taste, sans everything'. Okay, this plays into young people's fear and horror of age, but if the Covid pandemic has taught us anything, it is that the vulnerability of the elderly is a social crisis facing us all.

The fact that no government has yet resolved the problem of social care funding suggests they too prefer to hope we'll all stay relatively healthy until near the end, and our offspring will take care of us. The 2024 Terminally Ill Adults (End of Life) Bill, commonly referred to as the assisted dying bill, shifted the rhetoric about this subject, but its terms are so limited that it will affect only mortally ill people in the final months of life. A friend of mine, Sarah, whose husband of seventy-three died recently and who has three children and three grandchildren, was still caring for her mother-in-law who reached the age of 103. As we know, women – many no longer young – constitute the majority of carers carrying the burden of often intolerable chronic illness and suffering. Heartfelt stories from women such as these helped sway the bill's first reading debate in its favour.

'My Ghost, a magna opera of words'

I have been aware for many years that my own death will probably take place in a hospital or nursing home, attended by paid staff and not surrounded by children and grandchildren. As my partner and friends become ill, disabled or dead, there may be no one to sit at my bedside or arrange my funeral. I don't give a damn about the ceremony, though I do care to some extent about my legacy in terms of publications, books (many specialist and of significance to scholars), the paintings, friends' etchings and prints I've collected, and photographs, scrapbooks and journals. Will my writing and the memory of my teaching, leadership, festival directorship and more be remembered at all? Who will want any of my papers and memorabilia, or will it simply get thrown unceremoniously into a huge skip? And does it really matter?

I heard a new perspective on all this from a much younger woman than me, the poet Tania Hershman, who was appointed as writer-in-residence at Manchester's Southern Cemetery. In 2019, she presented a BBC Radio 4 programme, *Who Will Call Me Beloved?*[11] Aware this title might suggest self-pity or deep sadness, she counters immediately by saying she loves living alone without partner or children, but was struck by how many gravestones carry the word 'beloved'. She points out that these tributes indicate close family relationships (usually with husbands, wives and children) and so asks, 'Am I anyone's beloved, or do I need to be?'

Tania recalls the gravestones of women that don't suggest close relationships and have a lighter touch: 'in affectionate memory', 'inspirational', 'still not a morning person', and – one she saw in Cornwall – 'She had fun.' She interviews another poet, Helen Darby, who is confident that she is beloved of her friends and needs no 'advocate or friends' to organise her funeral and gravestone. Tania decides that the 'advocate' who will organise her gravestone will be herself. Inspired by Raymond Carver's poem, 'Late Fragment', with its line 'To call myself beloved', she decides to request a gravestone with only her name and dates – assured that notwithstanding there will be those who miss her. She is aware that a gravestone carrying loving and fulsome tributes, with tended flowers and plants from children and grandchildren, bears witness to a rounded life confirmed by that resonant term 'beloved'. As a childless poet she knows that *her* legacy will be her words.

For writers, the legacy of words is a compelling justification for having no children – though it imposes a responsibility to make use of their talents and childfree time. In her memoir *Manifesto*, novelist Bernardine Evaristo offers a strategy for creativity being valued, shared and passed through generations. She isn't a mother, and describes herself as 'childfree, as opposed to child*less*, which implies a failure to fulfil my role as a woman rather than an active choice not to have them'. She is both an aunt and a godmother, roles she claims to love. Following 'twinges of broodiness' when she went to festivals and saw 'adorable little wild-haired children running around wearing funky clothes', and coming from a large family of eight so she knew well the 'responsibility and unpredictability' involved in motherhood, she committed herself completely to her 'creativity': 'Writing became a room of my own; writing became my permanent home.' Defining herself first and foremost as a writer, she quotes Zuleika from her novel *The Emperor's Babe* when describing her legacy: 'To leave a whisper of myself in the world. / My ghost, a magna opera of words.'[12]

That idea of 'a ghost' is a familiar trope in the writing of Hilary Mantel, and I suspect she would have enjoyed Evaristo's allusion. In 2021, on the eve of the Italian publication of her memoir, *Giving Up the Ghost*, Hilary Mantel told an Italian newspaper journalist:

> When people interviewed me . . . they were searching for a story to fit me. 'Childless woman writer, devoted to art' is a popular story. But I did not like its confines and assumptions. I thought it would be best to take control and offer my own version of myself. I often had to say to people, when they offered some wonderful opportunity – travel, for example – 'I cannot do that, I have a long-term illness.' I wanted to add, 'I suffer from fatigue and I am often in pain – I cannot rely on my body.' But endometriosis is not a condition that you can explain in one sentence. For me, the condition and attempted cures have devastated my life. Many cases go undiagnosed for years, causing immense distress. I am glad to have played a small part in starting the conversation around the condition.[13]

She went on to say that writers often reproach themselves as being useless to society, but in this case, 'I hoped to do some practical good in the world and, more selfishly, I thought that writing about it might free me from the burden of making excuses.' Given the huge impact Mantel's memoir has had on women readers, with its excruciatingly detailed and precise evocation of the disease, that is quite a legacy.

For Bernardine Evaristo and Hilary Mantel, this notion of creative legacy is a matter of pride rather than conflict. The media, however, enjoy featuring creative women with tragic histories. In November 2021, under the headline 'Why I'm

GLAD I could never be a mum', the *Daily Mail* featured 'top novelist' Amanda Revell Walton (who publishes as Nancy Revell) describing how she was 'devastated when years of IVF failed' but had since realised she would never have 'achieved the professional success I have, or be living the life I do' – namely publishing twelve novels, most bestsellers, and having a TV drama in the pipeline, as well as a husband recovering from a serious cancer. Her story is designed to encourage other women struggling with failed IVF – her life has been possible *because* she doesn't have children – and to urge them to 'come out of the shadows, shed the guilt or . . . the feeling of being an outcast, and embrace the life we have all been gifted'.[14]

This is all very well if you have enjoyed a successful, lucrative career and/or have satisfying creative skills, a good set of relationships, and a comfortable home in which to live. What of women who have few or none of those, and may be part of an ethnic culture that prizes fertility, and who nevertheless are unwilling to have children – the badge of a 'natural woman'? What compensations can life offer them when others see them as unnatural, freakish, pitiable or child-hating?

Chapter 4

'Family Comes First': Other Women's Childfree Stories

I don't believe any researcher has done a significant study of the reasons women of different class, race, ethnic and religious backgrounds have chosen to be childfree. It's such a sensitive subject, especially for women in certain religious or racial groups and for those who've lived beyond menopause and now have no 'choice'. However, while writing this book, I had email, phone and in-person conversations with a number of women who gave me potted life stories and some thoughts on their childless/freeness. Interestingly, almost all asked me to use a pseudonym or abbreviated name.

What I discovered through those conversations was how complicated their choices had been, and how convoluted were the many different routes by which they'd travelled to become childless mature women. No one has a straightforward or simple life story, and there are many sad tales of abortion, baby loss, sterility, reluctant partners, failed IVF and adoption attempts, career demands and more.

As with many things in a long life, these women took false turns, ended up in dead-end relationships, put off making the big decision until too late, and/or had a major crisis which prevented their starting a family. Like me, many increasingly felt ambivalent about having no children, or in some cases harboured a deep regret for a decision that had seemed fine until their sixties or seventies. Retirement from work was often a shock as they realised they had a huge empty nest. The thread running through all their stories was the feeling of being an outsider, an observer of others' family lives – knowing that you will always be somewhat of an afterthought in your parenting friends' lives. 'Family comes first,' said my interviewee Rosalind Sanchez.

Despite that, middle-class childfree women are very aware of their privileged status, whatever the drawbacks. As Rosalind described it:

> I am acutely conscious that this is something which for me is only possible because I have financial independence, social status, an extremely rewarding and stimulating career and retirement, and close and loving friendships. These, I know, are not the norm for the majority of women, even in this country, never mind other societies and cultures. A friend recently drew my attention to the fact that having a child only very recently became a conscious choice. In my mother's generation, despite the existence of rudimentary contraception, I don't think it really was much of a choice.

So many women past middle age were born into families in which mothers had limited and unsatisfactory birth control, often having to bear unwanted children. Because of this, there's a childhood pattern of unhappiness, maternal reluctance or neglect which led them early on to resolve never to have children of their own. It's interesting to read their thoughts as older women, who obsessively focus on their own mothers and grandmothers as (anti-)role models and echo those women's perspectives on parenting. In the following recollections, the maternal ambivalence and unhappiness they experienced as children – at a time when to turn your back on motherhood was frowned upon – played a key role in their choices.

First, Rosalind on a mother and father sending out mixed messages:

My mother, who had three children in the space of four years, was an extremely anxious and overprotective parent. It may have been a response to my father who was pretty hands off and tended only to get engaged in extreme circumstances. So, looking back, I think I must have seen motherhood as an all-consuming, demanding, and not particularly rewarding role. Also, as an adult my father told me that my mother never wanted to have children, and this sent a weird message. Did he persuade her? Did she change her mind? Was it social pressure? Anyway, maybe it sent a message to me that there is a choice to be made.

However, despite evidently finding motherhood very challenging in the post-war period, my mother strenuously promoted the virtues of being a wife and mother to me and my sisters. She even picked out suitable men for me to marry. Her mantra was 'girls should become teachers, nurses and wives and mothers'. In her view, there were no other options. I can still recall feeling resistant to that pressure.

This demonstrates well how closely we women absorb our own parents' attitudes and resistance to all that is involved in parenting, and how confusing it can be when mothers adopt a very conventional line with regard to their daughters' lives. Clearly a product of her own time, Rosalind's mother suffered the fate of women who were 'consumed' by mothering, but who were nevertheless acquiescing to the social pressures on young women to take on conventional service jobs and become wives and mothers.

Another correspondent, Angelina, described to me a disturbed and dysfunctional family history, which made her resolve early on not to be a mother:

I decided very early on in my late teens that I would not have any children. The real wish to not transmit my DNA to another human being came from my maternal side. My mother left me when I was very young, I believe I was three years old. I was brought up by a great-aunt for a bit and then by my paternal great-grandmother until I was seven years old (when I returned to live with my father). But this formed part of a pattern for me, as my maternal grandmother left my maternal grandfather with two little girls under the age of five. My grandfather was a single dad in the early 1950s. I only saw my mother's mother once. And she was not interested, so it seemed a very cold and unemotional affair. I deeply felt that there was something amiss in my DNA and did not want this nonsense to continue.

And here is Nicky B, describing her mother's damaged and damaging relationship with a confused daughter:

My decision not to have children myself was a product of my own childhood experiences. As the eldest child of four, I was a first-hand witness of the unhappiness of my parents' marriage. When I was a few months old, my parents went to Cornwall on holiday. My mother invited a woman friend to join them as she could not bear the thought of holidaying alone with my father (and of course, the baby me). When we were older, my mother used to tell my siblings and me that family patterns were inevitably passed down from one generation to the next. It felt like the predetermined outcomes of Greek tragedies, irrespective of all efforts to avert catastrophe. We knew that she was referring to the damaging relationship she had with her own mother, and it was a message of deep despair. I realised that the only way out was not to have children because that meant I would not pass the damage on to the next generation. I think the depth and tenacity of my own decision reflected the iron fatalism of my mother's often repeated message.

When I was a very troubled teenager, my mother told me that I was a lesbian, that I hated men, and that I would never find happiness with a man. Many years later I asked her if she thought this was a suitable thing to say to a teenage daughter, and she replied 'Didn't you understand that I was working out my own difficulties?' I couldn't believe her answer – did she really think the teenage me was capable of such reflection when I was drowning in my own difficulties at the time? So clearly I was not a good candidate for motherhood even if that was what I wanted.

With all these women, and for me too, there is a deep fatalism about the generational repetition of negativity and suffering. We are deeply affected by the absence of a positive maternal role model and/or contradictory messages from grandparents and parents. And while some women feel the urge to react against traumatic or painful childhoods by marrying young and having children to counter or erase their family history, for others (like Angelina, Nicky and myself) the business of procreation seems too problematic or perilous.

Resisting Motherhood

Nicky's mother's words reflect the difficulties women have found in articulating their own dissatisfactions and sexual confusion. Despite Simone de Beauvoir's ground-breaking *The Second Sex* (1949), there was little feminist publication and debate in the 1950s and early 1960s, and critical public discussions of marriage and family life were thin on the ground. It was only with the appearance of groundbreaking books such as Betty Friedan's *The Feminine Mystique* (1963), Kate Millett's *Sexual Politics* (1970) and Germaine Greer's *The Female Eunuch* (1970) that women could begin to articulate our problems from a gendered perspective. I've already noted the impact on me of my first feminist tome, *The Feminine Mystique.* I read it through one long night, and sobbed with recognition of my mother's restricted life and my own attempts to escape that. For instance, Friedan points out that girls were prepared for motherhood by the dolls they received – and she cites Ibsen's 1879 play *A Doll's House* to show how infantilised women were in their husbands' homes and how wretched and depressed this made them (the much-quoted 'problem that has no name'). It had never occurred to me that dolls were intended to programme me for motherhood, and although I've already described my controlling love for my dolls that didn't lead me to maternal urges, this came as a revelation. The film *Barbie* brilliantly satirises this and reveals well the damage such dolls can do to girls' and women's selfhood.

It's interesting that three women I know who were adamant they didn't want children turned their backs on dolls altogether. Rosie B said her mother couldn't understand her indifference to the dolls she was given, and Rosie described her own feeling (not uncommon among the childless) that children only became interesting when they could talk. Audrey and her younger brother lined up all her dolls in the garden and threw stones at them. Bonnie G, raised in the conservative American Deep South, told me her uncle (who was clearly a southern man ahead of his time!) sent her and her brother Christmas gifts – a blonde baby doll for him, a toy pickup truck for her. Despite her parents' attempts to swap them over, she was delighted and insisted on keeping the truck and accompanying tools. A year later, when her parents gave her a Roy Rogers-themed pink cowgirl skirt and double-holstered pistols, she objected that what she really wanted was a turquoise-blue embroidered cowboy shirt and pistols: 'The Roy Rogers gear was much more interesting.' In Maggie Gyllenhaal's 2021 film, *The Lost Daughter*, a lost/stolen doll acquires layers of meaning, symbolising adult women's conflicted relationships with daughters. An old friend of mine, the scholar and poet Susan Castillo – raised (like Bonnie G) in Louisiana as a southern belle – wrote a poem about girls resisting dolls:

Rita the Walking Doll
When I was small I hated dolls,
My cousin Martha and I played with plastic horses.
They could run and kick and neigh,
Escape prim Southern parlours,
never said Yes ma'am.

One Christmas morning, though, a doll was skulking there
beneath the tree when I went down the stairs.
Her dress was stiff red taffeta,
polka-dotted white. Her eyes stared into space.
Her legs moved back and forth, but never swayed.

I hated her on sight. Later, one December afternoon,
my cousins and I were cowboys and Indians.

I played, needless to say, Comanche,
declaring warpath just like on TV, blood-thirsting.

And smiling, I scalped Rita.

Women talk of shying away from the drudgery of domestic
labour, the hard work and enormous responsibility of being
a mother. Tessa said her mother – who took a somewhat
distanced approach to her kids – felt she had given them too
much independence (of four siblings, only one went on to have
children). I suspect many mothers – like my own – regretted
their encouragement of a daughter's freedom which drove her
away from the family and often led to her becoming someone
from whom they felt alienated. Bonnie G, a depressed 'misfit'
who self-harmed, and was aware that her parents were deeply
unhappy, escaped her restrictive background and in 1969
went to a progressive university. That's when her relationship
with her parents became difficult: 'I was changing in serious
"alternative culture" ways of which they disapproved: bohemian
dress, political activism, and having "serious" relationships with
men they did not know or did not like when they met them.'
It was only after a furious row with her mother that her father
admitted to a longstanding affair with his boss's wife – helping
to explain why Bonnie felt depressed at home and anxious to
live a different life.

Several of the conversations revealed something I recognised
in myself. These women didn't feel they were up to caring for
a child for twenty-odd years, and they feared they would let

down any children they bore. Selfishness was something they acknowledged but it went deeper than that: there was a profound sense of insecurity and inadequacy to take on life's major job – and, as I've suggested earlier, the sense that they were still children themselves. But for some women, the decision was taken after much grown-up thought and discussion. Around her thirty-seventh birthday, Barbara E and husband Jerry went into a cabin in the woods to think it through. Both of them came from large families (she had five sisters, Jerry six siblings), all of whom were reproducing:

> Basically, I couldn't figure out any reasons to have children that weren't somehow selfish: Establish the relative immortality of descendants? Preserve your gene pool? Have someone to take care of you in old age? Create little images or projections of yourselves that would mirror you or recreate your childhoods for you? Create someone to love you, depend on you, make you special? Call it a failure of imagination, but nothing I came up with seemed unselfish. And there was also the environmental issue: children would consume vast resources. I could at least reduce my/our impact on the planet by a tiny degree. There was no need for us to add to the family and no pressure, even from my mother, who later surprised and gratified me by saying, 'You don't need to have children.'

Audrey told me her first husband wanted children, but after their divorce she and her second husband sat down every New

Year's Day to discuss whether or not to go ahead. Enjoying each other so much, they always decided against parenthood, though she suspects that if her husband had really enthused, she would reluctantly have agreed to comply.

The Attitudes of Others

Barbara E's sisters have conveyed 'a faint jealousy' to her. They are well aware that she and Jerry haven't had to spend money on schooling, clothes and toys, and have enjoyed more expendable income than all their siblings. She told me she feels that being a childless woman is 'a suspect condition, pitiable at best, selfish at worst, sometimes a bit enviable, but generally odd in a world implicitly structured as nuclear families'. And threatening to mothers, too. In her thirties, she was teaching a university Women's Studies course, including some challenging feminist texts about women's bodies. At one point, an older student walked out of the class, declaring loudly, 'I'm going home to my children.' This stung.

People's attitudes to childless women range from curiosity to hostility. It's often hard to know how you are seen, especially as lots of conversations on this theme are avoided, even if there's many a whisper behind your back. Those patronising words, 'You'll change your mind when you get older,' have been said to many young women (including myself). One woman, Ms X, told me her sister-in-law suspects she is jealous of her three children and life, and so makes her brood the centre of any conversation. Ms X is sure the sister-in-law is flaunting her superiority, a feeling one can often have when in the company of family members who may well envy the freedoms of single/ childless relations. She also told me that women friends talking anxiously about their kids would say, 'But you haven't had children so you wouldn't understand.' She finds this put-down irritating since, as she says, 'Perhaps I do so by looking through a different lens.' Penny said others feel she has missed out, and described herself as 'not part of the club'. Hilary Mantel told me she often detected envy, anger and condescension from women who have children, directed at 'perceived freedom'. However, Angelina feels she is 'an oasis' for mothers who are otherwise in some kind of competition with one another.

It's a common complaint by childless women and men that they have to cover for their colleagues during maternity and paternity leave, as well as school-run timings and children's sickness. Tara Wah, a sixty-seven-year-old obstetrician, told me she worked many extra hours to cover the maternity leaves of her hospital partner, who over fourteen years had eight children. 'She probably put more pressure on me than anyone else to have a child. I felt like an imposter when patients would come to me because they thought a woman would know what they were going through. I felt ashamed when I had to admit that I did not.' When asked why she had no children, she would tell people she and her husband were infertile, 'and that ends the discussion'.

Tania Hershman, whom I quoted earlier, feels childless women are perceived as very 'odd':

> There seems to be a greater acceptance of women who
> wanted children but couldn't have them. I felt – until I found

more women like me in my mid-forties – like I was a complete weirdo, there was something very wrong with me, the lack of that maternal urge. I feel I am not seen as a 'real woman' – the news constantly bombards us with descriptions of people as someone's parent, someone's grandparent. For example, if someone dies or is killed, it's 'Mother of three tragically dies . . .' etc. . . . , as if her death is sadder because she was someone's mother. I don't know, maybe it is sadder, I certainly feel for children who lose a parent, but I am interested in a person's identity not in relation to anyone else.

She described attending events in her thirties and forties:

I remember being at the Jewish circumcision ceremony for one of an almost endless stream of friends' baby sons, and a good friend – who also didn't have children but wanted them – almost shouted at me, 'Doesn't this make you want to have children? You'll regret it!' I also had a very odd experience being berated by a young gay man because I could have children and was choosing not to and he couldn't. I was at a dinner party once in my thirties where all the women started discussing their experiences of giving birth, which was fascinating, horrific and very alienating for me. I tended to always be the Only Woman Who Didn't Want Children everywhere I went during those years in that city. I would often get bored when conversations turned to talking only about what their children were up to.

For some women in the early days of the women's movement, there were serious consequences to speaking out. In 1974, New York author Marcia Drut-Davis was sacked from her teaching job after explaining on the TV programme *60 Minutes* why she didn't want children. Public hostility in the form of many death threats followed her dismissal, necessitating police escorts.

Regrets?

As women grow older, regrets can emerge, especially when surrounded by other women who are preoccupied by grandchildren. Karen, a singleton, told me she worries about who will take her to medical appointments, look after her when she's ill, and help her pack up and sell her flat when she's too frail to live alone. She has friends, but it's not the same:

> Listening to people who have children and grandchildren, they can always turn to them for advice and support – financial, practical household, health matters, technical . . . For example the number of times I've asked someone how they did something on their phone/tablet/PC and they say, 'Oh I don't know, my grandson/granddaughter set it up for me.'

For some women, the decision not to procreate has caused considerable pain – sometimes to their surprise. Often women express a love of children and a joy in spending time with them, so there is sadness that they don't have any of their own. Linda wishes she had been 'the kind of person who wanted children and had enough confidence and trust in myself and the world to have them'. Seeing friends' satisfaction and joy in their grandchildren makes her 'wistful', and she feels that having children must bring 'much comfort and a sense of the circle being unbroken'. Jane H told me she has never had a partner, and in her late thirties for a while she felt very sad. 'I have vivid memories of holding my baby nephew and feeling a physical pain in my stomach at the thought that I would not have children. This went on for around a year. Apart from this period, these feelings have not overwhelmed me.' Hazel – who describes herself as 'old, single and childless' (her parents are dead and she is estranged from her brother) – calls the instinct to reproduce 'the heartbeat of the universe' and says she has one major regret: 'that I have never and will never experience the unique and overwhelmingly powerful love between a mother and a child . . . a love that seems capable of moving mountains.' She feels like 'an onlooker, peering into the window of a sweetshop whilst knowing that you can't have the sweets because of your own life decisions'.

In her late thirties, Tessa – from a family in which several single women adopted children just after World War II – considered adoption and contacted organisations that would enable this. She said there were 'endless barriers' put up, including the requirement that she have a male sponsor who would have to commit seriously to the adopted child. She gave up her attempt. Tara discussed adoption with her husband, but his attitude, which she reluctantly accepted, was 'Why take on someone else's problem?' And while unable to understand her infertility patients' readiness to undergo desperate measures to have a child, she admits to having been 'a bit jealous of fecundity'. Rosalind said that after her beloved father died, she felt an urge to have a child: 'His death called forth feelings I didn't know I had; it was visceral, he was my touchstone and so I guess the transient feeling of wanting a child was part of that.' Losing a parent can generate an unconscious desire in a woman (not merely the childless) to restore the link to ensure family continuity. A close friend lost her adult son when she was in her fifties, and experienced a profound visceral yearning for another baby. After my own mother's death, I felt a deep sadness at having no daughter or son beside me.

For women who were sexually active before the 1967 Abortion Act, or raised in countries where abortion was difficult to obtain, there are many accounts of (illegal, botched, traumatic) abortions undergone when a relationship wasn't right, the timing was wrong, or the woman didn't feel able to tell the father. Bonnie echoed several women when she said she didn't regret any of the operations but has 'grieved for my overall level of disturbance and my sorely neglected self'. As with my abortion, there is a lingering feeling that those decisions – which seemed essential in particular circumstances – might not have been taken at a different time, and have sometimes brought on deep remorse.

Loving Children Who Aren't Your Own

Just because you don't want your own children doesn't mean you dislike them and have no time for those of others – though, as we know, children are not universally loved, even

82

by their parents. Women I know cherish the children in their lives – stepchildren, godchildren, friends' kids, younger work colleagues. Eliza spoke of her two step-grandchildren, feeling 'humbled they have accepted me as part of their family'. She said the experience had taught her a lot about 'patience, tolerance and respect for the young' but also the 'frustration of having to stand back when a little advice might have been useful'. Nicky cared for her sister's son and friend's daughter and described these relationships with great tenderness:

My nephew said [of me], 'She's more like a mummy isn't she?' which melted my heart when my sister told me about it. These days, he is an amazing adult I am so pleased to have in my life, as well as a connection to a younger generation . . .

I [once] lived in a flat above a good friend of mine and her daughter. I grew close to the daughter, who sometimes banged on my front door on Sunday mornings demanding breakfast. I knew that her mother appreciated a lie-in, so A and I would have breakfast together. It seemed an intimate and precious time alone together. At other times I would read to her before bedtime, and one of her favourites was a childhood book of mine called *The Dragon and the Jadestone*. When she had her own daughter, I gave A the book so that she could keep our tradition going. She remains close to my heart and I know I am someone special for her, a kind of informal godmother.

Having stepchildren and step-grandchildren is an experience that some women – like myself – have found a difficult but interesting challenge. Maggie married a divorced man with a daughter, and was very clear she never wanted to take the child's mother's place (especially when her husband died). Her second, widowed husband has two children and two grandchildren on whom he dotes, and she notes that they 'have priority over our relationship': 'I'm here for back-up. I am not trying to usurp a late wife's role . . . but it's not an easy situation for me. I have an uneasy relationship with my new stepdaughter; her mother-in-law fortunately fills the gap I cannot, because she is "motherly" and I patently am not.' Maggie gets pleasure from their company and watching their development, but she can't 'fabricate a relationship with these children just because they are his grandchildren'.

Maggie is a teacher, and when asked about her own family has got used to resorting to 'a series of catch phrases around the theme that as a teacher I love working with small children especially as someone else takes them home at the end of the day'. Mary E was told that a teaching colleague suggested to a senior staff member that, having no children herself, she was unsuitable to teach children. Jane, who became a head teacher, reported that the issue came up a lot with parents, some feeling that the best teachers had children themselves. She used to stammer through an explanation, but now she explains that being a good mother has nothing to do with being a good teacher. 'A teacher's role is not to parent a child ... To steal from *Goodbye Mr Chips*, when asked I replied that I had sixty-four children, all of them boys.'

One woman asserted to me that being a mother is different

from having children, and mothers can come in many forms during a life. She has mentored and cared for many colleagues of whom she is proud, and is regarded by a few as a 'second mother'. She's very close to their children, to whom she feels like a grandmother. Pictures they have made for her fill her house and office, and one of their baby pictures is in her wallet. Her pithy conclusion: 'I missed a profound experience without saying I missed a complete life.'

A Biological Dead End?

Reaching her seventies, aware of mortality, Eliza felt sorrow that there would be no custodian for her family memories and possessions, and that she had 'no obvious attorney for my old age'. After talking to a married childless friend who said she might regret having no child to care for her during her final years and end of life, single Rosalind realised this would also apply to her. And K wrote that having children was one of the few things in her life that was a missed opportunity: 'I also know that it means I end here, which is a sad knowledge. But will or does that dominate my thinking? No.' Barbara E told me that a young medical student described her as 'a biological dead end'. Her defiant response was that genes are hardly our most important contribution to human welfare. 'My question to that medical student would be, "Why should I continue my line, and does the circle have to remain unbroken? Is my life invalidated by having no biological successor? Can't I just be enough?"'

Chapter 5

My Family of Friends

Given that 'family comes first', what is the alternative to having children and creating a biological family? Does your definition of family embrace all those people who are – in Danielle Henderson's words – 'a cobbled-together group of friends and people I'm related to, all defined by the fact that I can count on them'? She cites her grandmother, older brother, husband and best friends. Bella DePaulo calls friendship 'the key relationship of the twenty-first century', while Susie Boyt says: 'For some, friends provide a pleasant adjunct to life's substantial relationships, a decorative flourish to family and romantic bonds; a comic strip, a ribbon bow, icing. For others, friendship plays a more structural role. It's the cake, the plate, the table and the floorboards. I am firmly of the latter camp.'[1] How well they express my own feeling that friends are as important as blood relatives.

As a child, I always clung to close 'best' friends in order to validate my existence, to ensure I had a sympathetic pal in whom to confide romantic and sexual yearnings and crushes (and a shoulder to cry on when all went wrong), as well as a chum with whom to exchange ideas, laugh and have good times. Without a sister, I tended not to share my most intimate feelings with my brothers, though I always valued the things we had in common: games, humour, political arguments, TV and film viewing. As I grew older, my brothers, boyfriends and lovers weren't enough, and the pleasure of having women and – mostly gay – men friends has indeed provided the 'floorboards' of my life. Never more so than when the second-wave women's movement coincided with my early twenties, and suddenly female friendship was not only a personal comfort blanket but also a matter of political significance.

In the US and then the UK, I joined women's groups, attended meetings to discuss our 'demands', marched with others on the streets for free childcare, contraception and abortion rights . . . all these actions elevated my friends to sisters and comrades, transforming even our most intimate confessions into important political statements – 'the personal is political'. At least, that was how it felt, and the growing body of writing, films, TV programmes and media coverage of feminist action such as the Miss World stage-storming in 1970 confirmed that sense of being part of something much greater than myself.

We all seemed to be in it together, and like many others I fantasised about a world of semi-shared homes (not communes – I was too bourgeois for that), children passed between us all unimpeded by possessive birth mothers and biological fathers, and eventually in retirement a palatial shared women's house where we'd all enjoy our twilight years with a swimming pool, library and extensive gardens.[2] The euphoric optimism of that time, boosted by spirited feminist polemic in books, films, TV and at high-energy demonstrations, promised a glorious countercultural future in which gender roles would dissolve, sexual partnerships would scorn jealous power trips, and society would be totally transformed by feminist campaigns and role models. I know, I know . . .

Of course, this didn't all happen, though some of it did. There's no doubt that ways of seeing women, developing female self-confidence, defining our roles and responding to our needs and demands – not to mention material gains such as more equitable rights at work, increased pay and promotion opportunities, advances in birth control, and so on – have progressed considerably since the 1970s. But so much remains to be done, while the position of mothers as carers and workers has barely shifted. Not surprisingly, given the radical programmes feminists urged, there have been major backlashes and backward steps, and many of us from those early days deplore the way the notion of 'liberation' has been cheapened or cynically misused. But in the mid- to late-1970s it did seem like the world was going our way, and we were all moving in a totally new direction. Not least in terms of the reimagining and restructuring of childbirth and family life. In her memoir of the 1970s, aptly called *Daring to Hope*, socialist historian Sheila Rowbotham captures the complexities and tensions of alternative lifestyles adopted by feminists to avoid living the patriarchal family lives of their/our parents.[3]

Divisions between Feminist Mothers and a Non-Mother

Although there were fresh ideas around mothering in the 1970s, British society largely resisted transformed models of family life and definitions of family (to include LGBTQ+ people), and as my 'sisters' began to have babies, Utopia seemed a distant hope indeed. I was around many women who were experiencing what Kate Christensen calls 'baby lust'[4] – a strong biological urge to procreate. Usually this was with a partner who was on the whole supportive, and so the communal rhetoric began to break up as individual women retreated into the coupled world of maternity/paternity. There were new crèches and mother and baby groups, but children were rarely shared or disciplined by a wider circle of parents and non-parents. I was rebuked by one mother, the artist Monica Sjöö, for asking her son not to take a bite out of each piece of food in my fridge; surely, she argued, socialist feminism should mean we shared everything we had. I was too scared to argue that her son was out of control and badly needed discipline. I joined feminist gatherings in women's houses where new mothers, holding tightly to their offspring, shared complaints about exhaustion, sore nipples and male ineptitude. The sights, sounds and smells of new babies alienated me. I felt like a friendly male priest or journalist, lurking in a room full of crying infants and weary mothers, relishing my freedom to wave goodbye and drive off to work or home. Though feeling inauthentic as a woman and guilty as a feminist, I had no envy of my fecund sisters.

I was, however, aware of the pain felt by those who were finding it hard to conceive or were experiencing severe postnatal depression. The burdens and pressures on 'real' women seemed harsh indeed. My closest friend at the time was Carol, a colleague's wife who had given up teaching to move with him to Bristol and have their second child. Although seeing her regularly, I didn't realise she was developing postpartum psychosis following her daughter's birth. My abiding memory of the dog days of our friendship was a visit I made one day to her house, sometime before she was clinically diagnosed. Her toddler and baby were miserably wailing and – through her own tears – Carol said how wretched and violent she was feeling and how she was doing her best not to harm them. I stood in her living room not knowing what to do, and she yelled at me, 'Couldn't you take the kids off my hands?' My feeble hesitation (terror, actually) resulted in her telling me to get out of her house. I fled, and didn't go back for a while. The awful thing was that, at that moment, she had reminded me of women like my mother and the poet Sylvia Plath who came near to post-partum breakdown. I felt powerless to prevent this highly educated, isolated and trapped woman having to deal with the maternal frustration and claustrophobia that seem an inevitable part of caring for very young children. Unless you have sufficient funds for paid childcare, that is. Almost none of my friends had nannies or regular childminders, especially as most of them had moved a long way, geographically, from their own mothers who might have done that job.

While intellectually and emotionally supportive of what Kate Chopin calls in her novel *The Awakening* 'mother-women', I felt our bonds slipping away. My concerns were my job, my love life, and a struggle to save enough money to put down a deposit on a property – at a time when people in their mid-twenties could just about afford to do this. My centre of gravity was different from theirs, and understandably they didn't have much time for my preoccupations. I probably imagined, despite all the challenges, they were blissfully self-sufficient in cosy family harmony, while they doubtless fantasised about my life as one of trouble-free hedonism. I'm not saying that women with young children relate only to one another – indeed, to me the tensions and competitiveness among them became increasingly clear – but the childless do represent a threat and an unwelcome challenge to women who have lost both personal autonomy and enough sleep.

As the years went on, the distance I felt between myself and those women increased. Several of my friendships went into freefall as I failed to support and connect sufficiently with them, and I was building an academic career that absorbed most of my time and energy. When I confessed to a wise colleague, a mother of three, that I missed my intimate friendships, she told me some of those women would welcome me with open arms when their marriages or partnerships failed and/or their children grew up and gave them more free time. This turned out to be true, to an extent. I was there for several friends through divorce or separation, and as we have all got older some have returned with a richer and more nuanced rapport. As one ages, the differences between lives become easier to deal with as we open up to disparate experiences, and lose that intense rivalry of younger adulthood. I was happy to listen to stories of their teenagers' angst, anorexia, anxiety about exam results, and druggy parties, while my friends had to endure my complaints about difficult colleagues and missed publication deadlines. All of us shared feminist political concerns and activism, worries about ageing parents and friends, as well as empathy and remedies for conditions such as cystitis, menstrual, menopausal and sexual problems, and the distress of ageing skin, thinning hair and shifts in our weight. But what I didn't share much with mothers were the delights in the progress of their growing children, and the pleasures and pains of seeing dependent young people developing into independent adults, with all the ups and downs of their leaving home (and sometimes coming back!). Now I am pleased to hear about grandchildren's new jobs, degree results or places in university, but I rarely know these young people and they remain rather an abstraction. I recently upset a good friend by muddling up the names of her two very different granddaughters who had both achieved amazing things.

In recent decades, on film and TV, the theme of friendship has been given greater prominence than ever – responding to audiences of all ages looking for new ways to live. From long-running TV shows such as *Friends* (1994–2004) and *The Golden Girls* (1985–1992), to one-off films and series such as *Bridesmaids* (2011), *The Queen's Gambit* (2020) and *It's a Sin* (2021), the support and comfort friends give one another is spelled out in ways that challenge the hegemony of biological family. *Friends* gave a new vocabulary and lifestyle to singletons; *The Golden Girls* offered role models for older women creating a retirement community. In *It's a Sin*, gay protagonist Ritchie Tozer contracts terminal AIDS and is taken 'home' by his homophobic parents, who refuse to allow his friendship group to visit. Heartbreakingly, he dies feeling they have abandoned him.

What has transformed friendships in the last decade or so, and especially since the Covid lockdowns of 2020 and 2021, is the way we all communicate. No longer are we sitting by old-style telephones and awaiting the postman; now we have mobile phones for calls and texts, and a whole range of social media. There are online friendship groups for motherhood, miscarriage, stillbirth, menopause, cancer and much else. I can text or WhatsApp any of my groups day or night, and be sure there'll be a reply within hours or even minutes. No detail of my life, however trivial or huge, need go unremarked – even if I am sitting home alone. This means that we all now have more 'friends' than ever, if fewer real meetings, and with luck can always feel part of a larger community. Sadly, we're increasingly aware of the malign influence of many of these modes of communication, which can target lonely people, especially children, intimidate and stir up violent feelings against groups and individuals, and make people feel threatened and vulnerable. Although I admit to spending a great deal of time online, keeping in touch with family and friends I rarely see, I wonder how this practice has shaped and will continue to shape my 'friendships' as technology evolves and I grow older. There is at least the comfort of knowing that, even if physical deterioration prevents me from visiting or inviting round those I care for, we can stay in contact.

The Networks of Women

In 2024, journalist Rachel Cooke published an anthology, *The Virago Book of Friendship*, by more than one hundred mainly female writers, in which she made a case for women's friendly communications being more frequent and richer than men's. Women have always worked hard at keeping friendships going, partly to share life experiences and build protective shields against a world designed by and for men, and partly to exchange solutions for practical and emotional problems and tasks, especially within family life. When researching and writing my book *Why Women Read Fiction*, I was struck by how many formal and informal groups women form in order to stay connected – mother and baby, walking and reading groups, coffee mornings, Ann Summers lingerie-selling evenings, quilting bees and more. And although these haven't been my groups of choice, I've been drawn to collective writing projects organised in women's homes, where the business of discussing and collating articles and books has been done around the cosy mess and chaos of domestic life with new babies and children. For me, that humanised those projects, even if sometimes it hindered them, and it also reminded me that being a mother doesn't mean you have to lose your intellectual life or focus.

In the 1970s, when feminist publishing was in its early stages, I was involved in two writing groups I mentioned earlier. In the absence of modern technology, the process of collaboration was unwieldy, involving snail mail, landline phone calls, travel to London, and sitting together at manual typewriters with

Tipp-Ex (type-corrector) in hand. The first group (comprising fine scholars: Michèle Barrett, Maud Ellmann, Mary Jacobus, Jennifer Joseph, Cheris Kramarae, Cora Kaplan, Rebecca O'Rourke, Jean Radford and Margaret Williamson) came together to produce a university conference paper on women's writing which challenged conventional as well as radical socialist interpretations of the Brontë sisters' work.[5] We met at Jean Radford's north London home, ate lunch and tea together, read one another snatches of writing, and peeled off into other rooms to discuss and type up drafts. At the conference, we stood in a row in the lecture hall and each read aloud one section of the paper. This was a formidable sight, and the power of women's collective voices was spoken about, especially by daunted male academics, for a long time afterwards.

In Bristol, nine of us got together to produce *Half the Sky*, the first-ever Women's Studies reader for use in adult education.[6] This scholarly group consisted of Liz Bird, Miriam David, Helen Haste, Ellen Malos, Marilyn Porter, Suzanne Skevington, Linda Ward, Jackie West and me. Not only a compilation of the research and teaching materials we had all drawn from our various subject disciplines in those early days of the women's movement, it was also a bonding exercise that sustained a group friendship over four decades. The book's flyleaf gives everyone's academic credentials, then: 'Between them they have eight children, two of whom were born during the preparation of this book.' So our family of 'sisters' gave birth to both a new book and real babies – a nod to the link many writers make between literary creativity and childbirth.

In *Why Women Read Fiction*, I described the ways women fall into patterns of collegiality and collaboration. We share reading experiences, swap books, and flock to book clubs – many of which have lasted decades and seen their members through a lifetime. I've noted the close links that exist between mothers, and especially women who have children around the same time – watching them grow up together, standing together at the school gates, and developing a special bond that can last for life. In 2009, I was asked to read some life narratives written by a group of three women who had met in London as young mothers in the late 1960s. Jo was a writer and historical monuments activist, Lesley the wife of a film director, and Linda an arts worker and revolutionary socialist. Between them, they had ten children and five grandchildren. Despite considerable class, economic, political and educational differences, disparate life experiences and long periods apart, they had remained close friends through four decades. They'd supported one another through miscarriages, abortions, separations, divorce, family deaths, physical and mental illnesses of themselves, children and grandchildren, and the challenges of their working, emotional and family lives. In 2005, David, the new husband of one of the group, suggested they write for one another detailed narratives of their lives through those relationships, so for five years they did just that. This project, which they called TRIO, deepened their friendship and helped them give shape to their individual and collective lives within the social history of the 'boomer' generation.

In 2010, Jo the writer died, but not before I taped an interview with the three of them in her cancer hospital ward. During a long and emotional session, to the awed surprise of nursing staff, they talked of what they meant to one another, and how much they had valued that mutual support through a lifetime's joyful and tragic experiences. They didn't see themselves as feminists – indeed, they hadn't participated in the 1970s women's movement and remained ambivalent about it. As wives and mothers they felt threatened by feminist rhetoric, which seemed hostile to their main concerns – children and family. But having faced appalling problems with patriarchal institutions and attitudes, they understood only too well the importance of female solidarity. I was slightly adrift in a very child-centred group who had dealt with many intergenerational problems: ageing and sick parents, the death of a son in a car accident, a deaf grandchild, another grandchild with Tourette's syndrome, and their own physical and mental crises. Interviewing TRIO, I was reminded of the burdens that mothers and grandmothers (as well as daughters!) have to bear to sustain and shape family life. I was also struck, as I interviewed them in that cancer ward, that they felt they'd saved one another's lives at crucial moments – so, as she died soon afterwards, Jo's death was a severe blow to a unique female triumvirate. The tape transcript was used later in a powerful staged drama about female friendship. Now that Linda has died, the transcript is even more valuable to Lesley, the sole survivor.

I myself am part of a 'trio' which began shortly after my seventieth birthday. My two oldest schoolfriends, Anne and

Lesley, share December birthdays, and when we all turned seventy, we booked a weekend break in our home city, Birmingham. Although we'd kept in touch over the years – with long gaps – we'd never met like this. The last time we'd shared the same space was the memorial service for Anne's son, an experience which had drawn us closely together. So, for two days and nights, we sat in a Lebanese café, a canal-side restaurant, the city's art gallery and its concert hall, sharing memories, ideas, gossip and reflections on our different paths through life. Anne and Lesley have between them four children and five grandchildren (in Lesley's case, step-grandchildren). After that memorable weekend, Anne set up a WhatsApp group for us – LAH LAH (after our initials) – and ever since we've posted almost daily. Through this, and regular Zoom meetings, we've been able to support one another at a distance over daily preoccupations – from partners' and children's serious illnesses to fences blowing down, our own hospitalisations, a stolen handbag, children's weddings, and problems with bunions, backache and breast biopsies. Photos go to and fro – of children and grandchildren, though also holidays and garden plants – and I observe the way my friends' timetables are determined by school half-terms and holidays, when they can unite generations. The awesome complexity of their extended family lives bedazzles me, though I admit to feeling relief that my own life by contrast can seem relatively untrammelled.

However, this has underlined for me how little contact I had with my grandparents. Very occasionally, my parents took us to see ours in the North-West. My father's parents used to run a shoe shop in Knutsford, and had what seemed to me a huge house (it probably wasn't) and a garden full of sweet peas, which I found magical so was encouraged to pick. My Boltonian maternal grandmother, who had been widowed and thus became destitute, was a live-in housekeeper to a wealthy man who died after some years, leaving her without a penny. She eventually came to live with my parents after I left home, but sat in her own room and was so timid and quiet my brothers and I can hardly recall a single conversation. When I read my friends' WhatsApp descriptions of joyous grandparental outings, trips to London and the north-west of Scotland, and long confessional conversations in which they offer advice and help to the younger generation about mental and physical problems, I realise what I've missed in my own past. Although Anne and Lesley engage generously with my concerns and activities, I do feel sometimes a spectre at the feast, writing rather solemnly about my adult-focused daily routine and pleasures in a way that lacks the special joy, humour and intimacy of relations with the very young. Having those young people in your life may remind you of your age and mortality, but it also keeps you in the loop of children's energy, optimism and playfulness.

I asked them both what LAH LAH meant to them. Anne said she really liked and valued its 'ordinariness', sharing the 'incidental everyday things which individually are often unremarkable but are a window into how I'm feeling and what's happening in my life . . . a way to keep in touch with you both and be able to share problems, difficulties and good times'. For her, the WhatsApp group 'is like a link between us that ebbs and flows at different rates with no pattern or expectations', including a visual element 'as photos add to the experience of living virtually alongside each other as we share our lives. It's rather wonderful.' Lesley agreed with Anne that conversations are 'undemanding', though with 'a depth in what we can express and it always feels honest and open'. For her, 'it is the trust that we will consistently be interested in each other at all levels, what we are reading, cultural events we have attended, and just how and who we are as three older women who met as schoolgirls and have loved each other over so many years'. She too values the photos we post of 'holidays, family and friends, gardens, new haircuts, bruised faces or hearing aids'. Both agree with me that sharing views on current political and social matters offers valuable fresh perspectives.

The Death of Friends

In the last two decades, I have lost a large number of friends, several in their fifties and early sixties. Cruelly, some of my dearest women friends have died of misdiagnosed cancer, and others recovered then – after remission – found the tumours had spread and there was no longer any hope. Several friends are now living with this appalling disease, and since the arrival of Covid in its many variants, I'm more aware than ever of human vulnerability and the possibility of untimely deaths. As friends have died, I've grieved over their loss, but also the loss of chunks of my own history and memories which have gone with them. Not memories of a world of families with children, but instead shared university experiences, intimate confessions about lovers, foreign travel, political engagement, collective writing, the deaths of parents and cats. And although I was deeply affected by the passing of my parents, the deaths of women who saw me through joys and trials on a daily basis over decades have hit me very hard indeed – though those deaths are never accorded the same value as *family* deaths. I was shocked to find, in Julia Samuel's acclaimed book, *Grief Works: Stories of Life, Death and Surviving*, there were sections on 'When a partner dies', 'When a parent dies', 'When a sibling dies', 'When a child dies', and 'Facing your own death' – but none on 'When a friend dies'.[7]

My first shocking experience of a friend's death occurred many decades ago. In the early 1970s, I went on an Educational Technology (early IT) course at Plymouth Polytechnic, to learn how to make tape-slide and video presentations for teaching Liberal Studies. Ann, the only other woman in the group, had come from Paris, where she worked for UNESCO and was trying to develop similar skills. We giggled our way through the two-week course at which we were both completely hopeless, cooperating on a pathetic tape-slide about flowers, and we became good friends, later exchanging hospitality in Bristol and Paris. After a long silence, she wrote to say she was coming to Bristol with her (secret) lover and wanted a discreet place to enjoy a weekend. My partner offered her his flat and we provided wine and food so they could enjoy each other in private without having to shop. After her return to Paris, we learned that she was – joyfully – pregnant, and because she had a great interest in medical literature she asked us to go to

Bristol's medical textbook shop and buy for her a whole bunch of books about pregnancy and childbirth. I duly mailed them to Paris and heard nothing more. One day, a mutual friend rang to tell me she'd gone into early labour, and while in the hospital had an aneurysm. She died instantly, as did the baby.

The shock of this, so soon after learning Ann was happily anticipating being a mother, was mitigated by learning her funeral would be in Bristol, where her father lived. We did some research around local funeral directors and found the date and time. Because I was teaching the day of the funeral, and knew my employer's permission to go would have been refused on the grounds she wasn't close family, I felt unable to attend – but instead sent flowers with a note asking her father to contact me so we could meet. Why on earth should he have responded to someone he didn't know? Of course I heard nothing more. We've never been able to find her cemetery plot. What I resolved after that was always to cherish my friends and make every effort to attend funerals. The absence of opportunity to grieve with others, embrace family members and friends, and find out more about who Ann was and exactly how she'd died, haunted me for a long time.

At the beginning of the twenty-first century, death was all around me. My father had died some years earlier, while my mother had fractured her pelvis and become disabled after being knocked into the gutter by a teenage cyclist. She was misdiagnosed by her GP, who said she had shingles. She went into a home, very unhappily, and died of a stroke in 2004. The year before, DJ and I had decided to get married, and booked a fortnight's pre-wedding holiday on Lake Como. This was a bittersweet time as three of our close female friends, two without children, were dying of breast cancer, a disease which – in a cruel twist of fate – is more common in childless women. All three were dead by the following spring.

One of those women was Kate Fullbrook, with whom I taught in Bristol for many years and had shared work and personal traumas. Never in fine health, she was a dedicated teacher and writer, and we exchanged writing drafts and swapped books. I liked the fact that she and her husband – both countercultural revolutionaries from the States who had come to the UK to escape the draft – were committed to their writing and their uncontrollable husky dog. Our conversations were fairly cerebral and I never directly asked her about having children – but I knew her partnership was very close and (perhaps because of the beloved husky) needed no third or fourth person to complete it. She phoned me one day in a terrible state to say she'd been to her GP because of a lump in her breast. He'd dismissed it and she marched up the hill to one of Bristol's private hospitals where she demanded to see a cancer specialist. He confirmed, after examination and a test, that she had breast cancer.

Kate was redirected to the NHS and underwent months of chemotherapy and radiotherapy, after which she lived for another couple of years until the cancer returned with a vengeance. Again, she undertook chemo, which made her very wretched, but it was too late. I feared she might die while we were on Lake Como. My last visit to her, the day before we flew to Italy, was to a grim basement cancer ward where – of all inconsequential things – we shared a short conversation about driving. I asked her why she was always such a nervous passenger, and for the first time she told me she'd been in a catastrophic car crash when in high school. No wonder she jumped in panic every time I braked when driving her anywhere. As I left the ward, I looked through the window and saw her tiny feet emerging from the blanket. That was my last sight of her. At our Lake Como hotel, I received a phone call from a mutual friend to tell me she had died.

After a private cremation, her husband and a few close friends met to scatter her ashes in a graveyard clearing near her home. A couple of years later, I was asked to give a lecture in her honour. In a lecture hall full of people who admired and loved Kate, I attempted to address our collective loss and also to celebrate the significance of her intellectual life – which, like mine, had specialised in American culture, transatlanticism, race and gender:

I'm focusing on a city to which the term 'loss' is alas all too appropriate: New Orleans, much of which disappeared under water following Hurricane Katrina during the first week of September 2005. Some commentators believed the city's soul had been lost forever. However, as with the loss of the individual we salute tonight, in New Orleans there is a profound and growing sense that the losses sustained have not killed off the spirit. Despite (and indeed, because of) the economic ruin and enforced diaspora that have followed the floods, there is a resurgent mood of regeneration and hope for the living and the parts of the city that can be rebuilt.

In that lecture I expressed optimism and hope emerging from devastating loss, hoping Kate's inspirational example would sustain us. I intended the comparison to resonate, but I can't say I felt it. While grieving for a city I loved, I knew that – unlike New Orleans – Kate (who like me had no religious faith) wouldn't rise again. All I felt was a dismal sense of the loss of another childless woman whose preoccupations had echoed my own.

From 2013 to 2017, four women who were significant in my life died, two of whom were in Bristol so I was heavily involved until the end. In each case, I visited, brought books and treats, and talked both inconsequentially and seriously. The role of the friend at a deathbed is difficult. You have none of the intimate closeness of long-term family members, yet are welcome as a friendly presence who can distract temporarily from pain and suffering. If you're lucky, friendships deepen towards the end of a life, as conversations expand from the trivial to the philosophical and spiritual. This happened in the last months of my friend Helen Dunmore's life. A distinguished novelist and poet, she faced death with astonishing courage and resignation (her Catholic faith helped a great deal), and until the last days of pain and weakness she was planting seeds in her garden and seedlings on her window ledge. I treasured and tried to keep alive the little deep-red nasturtium she gave me. Even more, I appreciated the remarkable poem she wrote about death on her iPhone in her final days. She emailed it to all of us in her poetry group, and it was later included in a collection of posthumously published poems. Helen's passionate love for her children, stepson and grandchildren taught me a great deal about the rewards of family life, as I saw how her maternal imaginative creativity fed into her writing and her whole life.

My most recent loss is Liz Bird – one member of the *Half the Sky* Women's Studies group – who died of lung cancer. A lifelong non-smoker, she had developed the disease over some time. However, because of her own stoical refusal to accept she was ill, and then medical blindness to her symptoms, she was diagnosed only four months before her death. Liz's decline was shockingly fast, scarcely comprehensible to her family and friends who knew her as exceptionally energetic and active. She was still doing Zoom exercise classes, walking the dog, printmaking, and standing up weekly for three hours in a life drawing class. During her final months, I visited her with crime novels and chocolate, and took her to an art exhibition and for coffee at a garden centre, but in the last weeks she wished to see only family – her husband, son, nephew, brother and sister. That 'family comes first' decree was strictly observed, and from early September until her death, I saw her only twice, briefly, to talk about mundane things.

When she died, I was asked to write a *Guardian* 'Other Lives' obituary. Gathering background and chronological information from her husband, son and siblings, I marvelled as I always do at the multifariousness of a person's life, the biographical trajectory you can trace from education through to early career, partner relationships and retirement choices. A holistic look at Liz's life was salutary: a fine research and teaching career, a contented cohabitation then marriage, motherhood of a devoted son, two grandchildren, and a post-career life as a printmaker.

I consulted the directions for submitting to 'Other Lives' – i.e. not famous people. The requirements are the obvious (date and cause of death, place of birth, etc.) but also names and occupations of parents, and 'survived by' – which means partner, children, and perhaps, especially if unmarried and childless, nieces, nephews and so on. Blood relations only. When I wrote my piece, I concluded by listing her family survivors, but I also wrote 'and her many devoted friends'. For we are also survivors. In many cases we have spent as much as or even more concentrated time with the deceased, and shared more activities with them over the years, than their siblings or close relatives. We, surely, are part of the family. That phrase was edited out of the final published piece.

Liz had a brother and a sister, but she was also *my* sister. We had been part of the women's movement in the 1970s when 'sisterhood' was the word used to describe our friendships through feminism. I know it seems outdated now, given the schisms and conflicts among different groups of feminists/women these days; how could anyone talk of a 'hood' of sisters? But for me, who never had a sister, that was how it felt – especially in our 1970s consciousness-raising group where we discussed our politics as lived in daily lives, covering work, money, family, children, our bodies and sexuality, and the challenges we faced trying to live as liberated women.

• • •

I've dwelt on some significant deaths of friends not to tug at my reader's heartstrings, but to illustrate how these can be as shattering as the deaths of close family members, and how as a friend I've had to cope with being just one mourner outside the immediate family, gently nudged out of the way or simply asked to speak at a funeral or memorial. I don't mean that my friendship wasn't recognised or appreciated; just that it was a secondary consideration while the immediate family (partner and children) threw a protective and defensive wall around the dying. But often at funerals the emphasis on family shifts in interesting ways. Apart from your own memories and experiences of someone, you learn about the patterns of friendships, acquaintanceships, formal and informal networks that sustained and enriched a life beyond immediate family. We know from research studies that a critical predictor of well-being and happiness is the range and quality of real connections or friendships individuals have, and that isolation and loneliness are key factors in depression and suicide. Far more men than women attempt and die by suicide, and their lack of close male confidants or companions is often cited as a reason. Instinctively, women have understood this, though out of necessity as well as choice we've relied on friends to help with childcare, emergency or chronic health problems, school runs, crises with young children and teenagers. Just as women are far more likely than men to ask a stranger for directions, so we are more likely to turn to friends or simply other women when in a fix or dilemma – be it a broken boiler or a bulimic daughter. Thus we help save one another's sanity and lives. Increasingly, films, TV dramas, novels and media discussions have focused on the importance of friendship, and on 13 February, the day before Valentine's Day, there is now a global holiday called Palentine's or Galentine's Day to honour friends and specifically women friends.

All that said, most of our friends must be treated with care, not taken for granted as perhaps we expect of our next of kin. We ask favours of friends – collecting prescriptions, watering the garden, offering a bed for the night, helping with moving home and so on. But even in the best of friendships we can't assume we have a place in their lives. Robert Frost's famous maxim, 'Home is the place where, when you have to go there, they have to take you in', doesn't really apply to *friends'* homes, even if in practice many of those friends would play their part. In material terms, we can't assume our centrality in our friends' lives. Most people leave legacies to blood relations, usually children, and the childless often name as legatees relatives who haven't been close but do fit the 'family' bill – such as nieces and nephews. I've never inherited anything from a friend, but I started to wonder whether I might name friends in my will. I was advised against it – partly because some of them may predecease me, and partly because I'd have to choose which ones merited most, and who would inherit my precious collections (of little monetary value) of books, jewellery, quilts and artworks. I considered a codicil instructing all my dearest friends to descend on my home after the funeral and take whatever they fancied, but a solicitor frowned on that and pointed out the possible chaotic scrum that would ensue. So, like many a childless woman, I will probably leave legacies to family members and the rest to charity. It seems family does indeed come first.

Chapter 6

Being Mothered

In that much-quoted poem beginning 'They fuck you up, your mum and dad', Philip Larkin traces with bleak cynicism the way generations influence and, in his view, hand on misery to one another. His suggestion to 'Get out as early as you can / And don't have any kids yourself' is a pessimistic and misanthropic response to the human condition.[1] I remember reading this poem as a teenager, feeling grateful for the words supportive of my own reluctance to have children.

The way we are parented has a large influence on our decision about whether to parent ourselves. I'm aware there are many people who were adopted or fostered, and never knew their birth parents, or whose parents died or rejected them when they were young, and for them the decision must feel painfully complicated. But for those of us who had parents into and through adulthood, the role models, encouragements (or not) and exhortations they provided were crucial in our own decisions about parenting. Was my response to Larkin's words confirmation of a desire to throw off parents, heritage, family ties that felt restrictive? Talking of getting out 'as early as you can' undoubtedly spoke to my itchy feet pointing away from the family home into a life of self-determination. Deciding not to have kids myself was one way of ensuring I didn't follow in my mother's footsteps, especially as she didn't want that – and she frequently repeated sentiments similar to Larkin's. But had I really broken away, and how thoroughly did I dissociate myself from a family and heritage that made me what I was?

In her memoir, *The Soul of a Woman*, Isabel Allende claims, 'Many of us daughters have had to live the lives our mothers could not.'[2] While this is increasingly difficult for young women with limited funds – facing exorbitant rents, modest pay and the huge costs of childcare – the aspiration of most is to live a better, richer life than that of their mother. Often this is supported by the mother herself who, like mine, wants her daughter to avoid the constraints and sadnesses of her own life and instead soar to the heights of success and happiness she failed to reach. Not surprisingly, this can create a tension between a mother whose life may have settled and stalled in certain ways, and the amorphous, indeterminate aspirations of her daughter. Ironically, with the cost-of-living and housing crises of recent years, that daughter may well look at her mother's situation – however mundane or unhappy – and see financial and domestic security that she fears will never be hers. Thus there is bound to be some envy, resentment and worry as the daughter wishes to wend her own way through a new life beyond the mother, though she may have to live for a time with her parents to save money for a property deposit and postpone adult autonomy.

In the past, when women could more easily leave the family home, many women writers from Simone de Beauvoir to Deborah Orr explored the tempestuous quality of this uneasy relationship.[3] Margaret Forster's mother was not alone in worrying about her clever daughter's 'striving' ambition, which she knew would produce a 'gulf' between them: 'What was I, so keen, so expectant, going to think important? What was I going to become if not a wife and mother?'[4] Although not keen for me to become either of these, my mother was aware of a similar gulf. And it was only after she died that I realised her constant expressions of anxiety and trepidation about my activities, plans and relationships came not simply from the critical stance I heard, but also from a deep loving concern that I usually brushed off.

When I look back, I realise how much I wished to be mothered – and how various mothers in my life responded. Apart from my mother Ida, I sought out female teachers, colleagues, colleagues' wives, and friends who recognised my neediness. When I briefly went into (classic midlife) therapy in my forties, the psychiatrist kept suggesting my parents admired and were in awe of me, but failed to give me the overwhelming love I craved – with the result that I was unable to imagine giving love to a child. When I began to write this book, I wondered how true that was, and decided to explore the matter further through documents and letters I'd kept for years but never reread.

In her mid-eighties, unable to take care of herself any longer, Ida Taylor moved into a residential home. My brother Geoffrey and I sold her flat and had the painful job of clearing out all her stuff. Since Ida once worked as a secretary, she had already decluttered but had carefully saved in chronological order a pile of papers, diaries, notebooks and scrapbooks. What I found, to my surprise, was a box full of my letters to her dating from 1968, my second year as a student at University College London. There were dozens from that time, then even more from the two years I spent living in Baton Rouge, Louisiana, taking an MA and beginning a teaching career, and finally a smaller number from my more recent years back in the UK, teaching first in Bristol then at the universities of Warwick and Exeter. I brought them home, piled them into file boxes on top of my bookshelves, and wondered if I'd ever read them again.

At the same time, also on my shelves, was a heap of letters written to a New Yorker, Louise. She was only six years younger than my mother and had befriended me when I first arrived in the US, continuing to give me hospitality and support while I lived there, then for many years after I returned to the UK. I regarded her as a second mother. Like Ida, my birth mother, Louise – also a secretary – had saved my letters in date order, and sent them back to me some years ago at my request. To my shame, in my travels I seem to have lost or discarded all their letters to me, especially Ida's which I recall were beautifully written.

My First Mother

As I planned this book, inevitably I thought a great deal about my mother, the way I was mothered, and her role in encouraging me not to mother. She has now been dead for over twenty years, and I think about her daily – though when I recall our times together and our conversations, I realise my memory is fading and playing tricks. What I do know is that I feel simultaneously loving, grateful, guilty and tortured about our relationship, and so it was with some misgivings that I reread my correspondence, to see how I had presented myself to her, and to get clues as to how she had related to me at a distance.

What embarrassed me was how incredibly self-serving and pompous all my early letters were. To my relief, I noted that in later years, the tone became more subdued and engaged with her news and the wider world. As a London student, I was anxious to boast about my frenetic social life, with a relentless emphasis on the men who were interested in me, the fellow students with whom I went regularly to the Golden Egg café for pancakes, and a rather sketchy description of my English degree course. I suspect this was partly to reassure her I wasn't the earnest bluestocking she had once expressed fears I might become, but much of it conveys self-aggrandisement and exhilaration that – after years at a girls' grammar school – I was part of a gender-mixed world in an exciting city. These letters veer between defiant claims of how well I was handling my seminars and essays and 'boyfriends', and humble entreaties for a little money, some recipes, blankets and sheets for my freezing flat. Touchingly, my mother responded promptly to all such requests, even sending a tin of home-made gingerbread men for an American fellow student who was enchanted by them.

The depressions, anxieties and disastrous times I had as an undergraduate are skated over in favour of accounts of parties,

Dramatic Society productions, student balls and journalism – tempered with quoted words of praise for and from my tutors and the odd reference to slogging through *Beowulf* in the Anglo-Saxon language. The regularity of my letters, my sadness when her and my father's occasional missives didn't turn up, and the joyful tone of my narratives of university life, in retrospect look like reassurances that my parents' financial sacrifices so their children could go into higher education were well worth it. I assured them I was rising to every possible challenge.

Only once do I write about an encounter with a man that went wrong (though there were many others), and that was because the man in question was the thirty-five-year-old teacher of my younger cousin, whose mother, my aunt Renee, I often visited. Sharing an enthusiasm for theatre, we went on a date but, in my account to Ida, 'he stopped his car and tried to seduce me, not accepting I was tired and wanted to go home. He wrestled with me. It was awful. No, don't worry – he didn't manage anything, but it really upset me. I had to hit him until he drove off.' That wasn't the end of the story, because the next day – to my horror – he rang to ask me out. Did I tell my mother this rather alarming tale because he was clearly a good friend of her sister's family, or to show how brave I could be under duress? My mother had told me as a teenager about a time when she was lured into the stockroom at the bank by the manager for whom she worked, so perhaps I was letting her know I now knew how she felt. Of course, I never wrote about my consensual sex life, even though – as I've explained – she had been privy to my abortion so knew I was no virgin. But never again did I tell her of the sexual harassment and assaults I experienced, largely because of my own shame and sense of personal responsibility (that familiar feeling for women of my generation – and, alas, subsequent generations – that I 'asked for it').

Moving to Louisiana

In 1969, I went to study in Louisiana and my letters were even more frequent and detailed than before. I was trying to emulate an ambitious young foreign correspondent informing her peers about an exotic and strange world, explaining what the Deep South felt like to an urban Englishwoman. There were details of crayfish boils, campus football games, sorority and fraternity houses, Spanish moss, the perfume of magnolias and dazzling azaleas, huge cockroaches in the bath, mosquitoes and high humidity, as well as the political horrors of war in Vietnam and racial segregation. I sent home an article about this strange world that got published in a Wolverhampton newspaper, hoping to be commissioned to write more (it didn't happen).

In my first semester, as I revelled in the fact that everyone on campus was fascinated by my Englishness and kept asking me to talk with that 'cute accent', I was suddenly a bit of a star. I had brought all the wrong clothes, sent a trunk of books and possessions by sea that took months to arrive, had almost no money, and was initially sharing a graduate dormitory room with a 'Georgia peach' who told me her grandmother said she'd die if Ann married a Northerner ('damned Yankee'). I understood without being told that she'd also die if Ann married an African American. Two new friends drove me to Walker, Louisiana, to hear bluegrass music in a hall covered with posters for segregationist Alabama governor George Wallace and the Ku Klux Klan. I wrote to my mother, 'It's really good to hear you say you feel close to me by sharing my experiences, as that's exactly what I'm trying to do.' What I tried to avoid saying was that I was terribly homesick, worried about money, bewildered by parochial small-town attitudes – especially towards African Americans and women (one professor called me 'our nice London lolly') – and wanted a connection with a mother who would be impressed but also empathise with my loneliness.

She didn't disappoint. For a start, as when I was studying in London, she sent me M&S sweaters, dresses, knitted caps (the envy of my friends), her scones recipe, and some of her own medications for the bad thrush I kept getting. While commenting on all I was doing and seeing, she offered advice about my emotional state. After a few months, she responded to a 'despondent' letter, and I replied: 'Your comments about my emotional life were painfully accurate ... I do manage, though – I don't go to pieces here, I manage to maintain my strength and cheerfulness – so don't feel sorry for me.' In a letter written after I'd described the joys of Mardi Gras with a pop-singer boyfriend, she picked up worrying signals, offering 'detailed and frank comments and advice' about my personality. I responded, 'You're probably right – I do have an inflexibility and a harsh tendency to criticise and be intolerant, though I try to control it as much as I can ...'

A month later, after feeling so jealous of her description of a familiar family favourite supper, beef and peach sandwiches, I wrote to say I'd decided to return to the UK because I was missing home and was very low on funds, as well as feeling there were 'so many things here to which I can only half-relate, or which seem meaningless to me' – though it seems my parents were by then wondering if I was living in a world of drugs. 'Don't worry about heroin and suchlike. I'm taking good care of myself.' Their hunch was shrewd, as I was indeed moving among people who took certain drugs for granted – cannabis, LSD, psilocybin, amphetamines – though fortunately not heroin. This was an exciting new experience for me, so I tried them all, but after a couple of bad trips limited myself to marijuana and amphetamines – the latter so I could write essays through the night. Yes, I did inhale, though I never shared this with my mother in my letters or later. It was only one of the secrets I kept from her.

I wrote a few days later to say I'd decided to stay in Baton Rouge. It was at this time, May 1970, even in a conservative state and campus, that I was meeting left-leaning people engaged in anti-war and anti-racist movements – so I'd found a reason to stay around. And while I suggested my mother read James Baldwin (I knew she'd never encountered African American writers, though she did read Indian and African novelists), she wrote to ask if I'd read Virginia Woolf's *A Room of One's Own*. Looking back, I see that we were both trying to impress and educate each other. However much my mother criticised and repudiated the women's movement throughout her later years, she was clearly influenced by women writers and thinkers, and even at a huge physical distance wanted me to share that.

New York and Hollywood

That summer, I went to stay in New York with my new friend Louise. After recently moving to the city, she was renting a studio apartment in Midtown Manhattan, so I slept on the floor in a sleeping bag for a few weeks while working as a waitress in a steak bar, accumulating generous tips that would pay for a West Coast holiday later on. While there, I met an actor called Perry, and was very quick to tell my mother I had fallen deeply in love (I'll spare you the saccharine descriptions). Perry's second cousin was the actor Shelley Winters, and in mid-August he and I flew to Los Angeles to stay for a few weeks in her Beverly Hills house, where the Actors Studio director Lee Strasberg lived in the apartment above. This gave me eye-popping insights into the world of Hollywood, stardom and great wealth.

Shelley herself was a clever, witty and politically engaged Democrat – and the first person to ask me what I knew about this new movement, Women's Liberation, and how she could find out more about the National Organization for Women (NOW). I hadn't a clue. She took me along to a TV show in which she was interviewed with a woman from HOW – Happiness of Womanhood, one of the first anti-feminist groups to get national publicity. I can't recall the details, but writing to my mother I said that Shelley had 'demolished' her. This impressed me, and I started to look around for feminist books and magazines, so ironically the seeds of my intense feminist activity were sown in Tinseltown. I returned to my degree course and teaching in Baton Rouge, where I picked up a copy of *The Feminine Mystique* and realised my life would never be the same again. Flying to New York for Shelley's Thanksgiving party later that year, I shared with her some articles and papers about the new movement. My relationship with Perry, however, soured; to some men, there's nothing more off-putting than a feminist zealot, and so our sweet romance and my high-flying showbiz life were over.

During that summer, my mother had written to tell me about friction surrounding my younger brother Richard's engagement to Lynda; my parents considered them too young and this caused a huge family conflict, which soured relations for many decades. I felt threatened myself, knowing how easily influenced I was by her and fearing that any choice of partner might cause similar criticisms. Indeed, my mother warned me against the relationship with Perry even when it was at its height; she was right, of course, that he would have been a disastrous son-in-law, but I also saw this as a blow against my independent choice and judgement. Once he was out of my life, however, I reverted to my customary bravado to tell her about 'liberation' speeches I was making on campus that I boasted were 'building up a lot of confidence in myself ... Your little girl is at present the campus heroine, invited to speak to classes and groups and leading marches and protests, and now teaching key texts such as Henry James' *Daisy Miller* as "a liberated woman's novel".' When I went with other women to one of the earliest NOW conferences in Houston, I wrote ecstatically, 'Oh Mother, I wish you could have been there to see some of those women, working day after day to change the iniquitous legal situation of women.'

I was fired up, not least because I was asked to draft a pamphlet outlining the lack of rights for women in Louisiana, under the Napoleonic Code. This ruled, among other things, that community property in a marriage was controlled only by men; women were not entitled to spend their own earnings without a husband's permission; no accounts could be opened without his permission; and women were automatically exempted from jury duty, with alimony laws loaded in men's favour. I cringed to read my patronising words of congratulation to my fifty-four-year-old mother for getting onto a teacher training course at Dudley College: 'I really feel proud of you . . . as a good liberationist I have to say you're a credit to our sex!' I banged on about my new resolution never to marry, quoting Germaine Greer (to whom I was compared on campus) and assuring Ida that she'd be fascinated by hearing about liberation and receptive to all its implications. Oh, the arrogant certainties of youth . . . Perhaps fending off my new-found obsession, she replied curtly that there wasn't much interest in women's liberation in the UK.

Going Home

I returned home in late August 1971. With unusual pre-science, I wrote that I suspected 'meeting me again in the summer may be somewhat of a shock to y'all . . . I have gone through so many radical changes since being here.' I also mentioned the fact I'd grown my hair very long – something I knew they wouldn't approve of – so I was already preparing for future parental arguments. But in the meantime, I had another awful shock for them. As part of the campus Women's Liberation group, two psychiatrists ran a 'sensitivity retreat' for women only (of all ages). It was an intensely powerful session in which we were encouraged to speak about our parents, partners and children, to scream, cry and wail, and explore our feelings about sexuality, marriage and family, and the way others saw us. It was an alarmingly theatrical weekend, with some women declaring they would leave their husbands or quit their jobs. For me, it was somewhat apocalyptic. Asked to speak the words my father Eric would use to describe me, I found I couldn't do it as I realised I had no idea what he thought of me, and I collapsed dramatically on the floor in a fifteen-minute fit.

This incident shook me to the core, and I told the psychiatrists I wanted to understand what had happened. They got me into regular group therapy for the next couple of months; during this short time I never got to grips with the meaning of my traumatic experience. However, in my view disastrously, the psychiatrist urged me to write to my parents to explain how this therapy was helping me understand my mini-breakdown as an 'identity crisis'. So I did, telling them I had 'released all kinds of hostility, resentment and childish anger which had been building up over years'. I went on to say my desire for achievement and success was directly related to 'an attempt to please and satisfy you' and that what my therapist had urged was: 'I must decide what I want for myself, even if I have to hurt you in the process.' I find this so painful to write about now, as guilt and bitter regret overwhelm me when I think of how bewildered my parents (who knew nothing of American psychotherapy) must have felt receiving my letter. Ida responded in very hurt tones, though generously – acknowledging that I would inevitably see their lives as very narrow on my return. But she pointed out the allowances and sacrifices they'd made and the help they'd always offered me. Ida then gave me some good old-fashioned advice, saying I should count my blessings. In a contrite mood, I decided to do just that.

After my return from the US, our relationship went through a rocky patch as I was determined to assert my independence and not rush into a safe career such as school teaching. Ida insisted I cut my hippie-ish long hair, but generously offered to let me live with them for a year or so while I did teacher training. However, probably with very bad grace, I declined and headed straight for London, where I did temporary secretarial jobs and then worked for a publisher for a few months, determined to have some fun after years of academic study. Then, encouraged by a friend, I applied for a lectureship at one of the new polytechnics, and to my astonishment got the job – so I moved to Bristol, where I have lived on and off ever since. As one of three young women (Carol Dyhouse, Madge Dresser and I) appointed to the old technical college incorporated into the polytechnic, we faced offices in 'terrapins' (prefabs with rotting window ledges and inadequate heating) with no women's toilets and the discomfiture of middle-aged male tutors who both found us desirable and dismissed us intellectually. It was here – teaching Liberal Studies to Biology, Commerce and Construction students while designing Humanities degree courses – that I experimented with Women's Studies and found my intellectual feet. The euphoria I'd experienced in the US was now replaced by more sober reading, writing and teaching, and I quickly discovered a 'sisterhood' of my generation who shared my intellectual passions, as well as struggles with patriarchal resistance in their work and home lives.

Margaret Thatcher and Family Tensions

I discussed some of this with my mother, and over the years – even though she was wary of the women's movement – we exchanged ideas and book suggestions, and had many an argument about politics. From the mid-1970s onwards, as I was an increasingly committed socialist, my mother became enamoured of Margaret Thatcher and proselytised on her behalf whenever we talked. Family gatherings – often fraught and difficult – became painful for me, as both my parents and brothers mocked my ardent and admittedly self-righteous left-wing self. My mother's nascent and conflicted feminism, manifest in an enthusiasm for women writers and support for women having careers rather than children, found a heroine in Thatcher. Ida admired her smart dress and coiffure, her brisk efficiency and her straight talking (all qualities Ida shared). In her last years, she stuck a huge poster of the ex-Tory prime minister on her wall – which I must admit to seeing as a provocation. In one letter, trying to rationalise our frequent arguments, I wrote,

'I do wish we saw each other more. I agree with all you say. [I don't know what she said but can infer!] Seeing each other so infrequently makes for a kind of awkwardness and shyness ... I wish we were nearer so we had more casual everyday contact.'

Some years later, when I was working 170 miles away and visiting even more infrequently, she told me with some sadness that what she would like was for me to pop in for twenty minutes daily, rather than for three hours every couple of weeks. I wearied her, and we found those visits hard to sustain. However, we retained that good reciprocal correspondence in which we shared practical tips and advice, and bolstered each other's confidence. In 1990, I wrote to praise the appearance of the house and garden, and noted how much she'd achieved in her 'considerable life's work ... there's no reason for self-deprecation'. I later advised her to get trainers for her always-problematic feet (something we shared), sent her a bottle of Olbas oil for her chest, and urged her to go on holiday. I asked if she was eating enough and suggested acupuncture for her feet and my father's sinuses. She was pleased to hear that, after years of unsatisfactory contraception, I was getting sterilised. In 1992, a year before my father died, when he was very ill and largely bed-bound, I wrote that she was 'bravely facing difficult times with great flexibility and good humour'. She had become an active humanist, and she sent me a humanist booklet about funerals, asking me – when the time came – to conduct hers. I told her this made me very tearful, and in the end I was unable to do it.

Ida's Final Years

My ties to Ida became closer and yet more fraught in the years following Eric's death. She needed help with her new flat with its various problems, and with paperwork for probate, bank details, and other administrative tangles, besides sorting out a new independent life. Years of caring for a sick man had taken their toll on her health – which had never been robust – and on general election night, 1 May 1997, at home in Bristol, when I was putting champagne in the fridge in preparation for what we hoped would be a Labour victory, the phone rang to tell me my mother (who'd had a bad fall) had collapsed and was in Selly Oak Hospital. I raced up the M5 and went to her side; the hospital then discharged her and we returned to her flat, where I put her to bed and watched TV until the early hours. In the morning, when I was weeping with joy as I watched Tony and Cherie Blair entering Downing Street, my mother's comment was: 'Oh no, now there'll be big union trouble and bodies will go unburied.' Rarely had our political differences felt so raw and alienating.

There were heavy pressures on Geoffrey and me following her hospitalisation as, unable to cope physically, she had to be readmitted, and for the last six years of her life she had multiple hospital stays, falls, and finally admittance to a residential home, which she hated. I had moved to work in Exeter by then, so I was unable regularly to clean her flat, do shopping and little errands. She described herself as 'livid' about my new job, which meant less frequent visits. Although this made me sad, I wrote a note to myself that I'd 'saved my own life by putting more distance between us'.

In 1999, we both attended my aunt's funeral in Ludlow. Married to my father's older brother, she was a writer and broadcaster who had always encouraged me to write and aspire to an intellectual life, something by which Ida felt threatened. Indeed, Ida shrewdly told one of my cousins, 'Helen would have liked Muriel as her mother'; there was a small element of truth in this, though I always preferred my mother's grounded native intelligence and sense of humour. My aunt had lived a privileged middle-class life, whereas Ida's struggles to escape from the disadvantages of her class and economic position were my inspiration for lifelong feminism. But my mother's words revealed her own insecurity and feeling of distance from – and perhaps some disdain for – the woman I'd become. She never wanted me to be 'ordinary', least of all a wife and mother like her, but paradoxically – apart from Margaret Thatcher – she feared and didn't warm to intellectual and politically engaged women.

Like me.

Diaries

In another box of my mother's papers, I found some of her diaries, the entries written religiously every day, recording five or six lines of events, visits, bowls matches, physical problems, TV programmes she'd enjoyed – and every phone call and visit from my brothers and me. For twenty years I avoided reading her last entries, dated December 2003 and January 2004, written before she died on the 26th of the latter month. I anticipated words of anger or – worse – indifference about my last disastrous visit to her in the residential home before she had the stroke that almost killed her. I had driven from Exeter to Birmingham expecting to do shopping and other little jobs. She was unusually cold and distant and complained she had nowhere to store her shoes. I said I'd go to Timpson's and buy a shoe rack, but she exploded with rage, saying I'd never been of any use unlike my brother Geoffrey, who she knew would easily do this job. She told me to leave, which with great reluctance I did. I drove away, but stopped the car round the corner tearfully to take stock. What had I done, and why did she always make me feel inadequate or useless? After years of ringing her daily, I didn't do so for almost a week, then relented and we patched things up – if a little awkwardly. The next time we met was in Selly Oak Hospital after she'd been revived from that first stroke.

So, twenty years on, I plucked up the courage to read the entries for the last couple of months, to see whether this contretemps featured in her diary. And yes, it did. On 27 December, she wrote, 'Helen at 11.45 – sorted out my Xmas presents situation for me. I was not on good form so I encouraged her to leave at 1 o'clock.' On 2 January, she recorded: 'Helen rang – loving atmosphere between us again, thank goodness.' Four days later, she recorded my brother's visit and my next phone call: 'Happy talk with her. How little they know of the hideous position I'm in.' Her last entries, describing bad falls, lack of confidence about moving around, pain in her back and endless sleepless nights, expressed terror of what would come next, and a fervent desire that it would all be over soon.

To her credit, in all the visits I made, she rarely spelled out how physically desperate she felt – though her depression was palpable – and always presented herself in a most dignified way, neatly dressed and made-up. All she would say to me was that she had lost mobility and physical confidence, and no longer wished to stay alive, even for our sakes.

Diana Athill said that the process of dying is made easier because of the presence of a daughter, and – despite living in a different part of the country from her dying mother – she was able to be present at the moment of her mother's death, receiving a beautiful smile of love and even hearing her mother's last words about how 'absolutely divine' her recent visit to a nursery garden had been.[5] My own experience of my mother's death was miserable. I had visited her a few times in hospital after her stroke, but the last time I was there she looked so frail and exhausted that I hung around until she asked me to go, saying there was nothing I could now do for her. We embraced, and I went back to sit in my car in the car park, wondering if I should go back and just be with her. I thought she might shoo me away again, but I've always regretted not going. The nurses knew how near death she was the morning she died – they told me afterwards that uncharacteristically she'd failed to put on her lipstick – but they didn't ring me. My brother visited that afternoon, but she died in the evening without either of us present. I felt intense jealousy of her friend Maureen, who told me later that she had taken fruit yogurts into the hospital ward as my weakening mother enjoyed being spoon-fed that sweet treat. Why did I not think of doing that?

Letters and an Autobiography

Reading through all my letters and my mother's little notebooks and diaries, I realised that in many ways the most stimulating and long-lasting elements of our relationship came from mutual writing and correspondence. When I was a student in England and later the US, our letters shared the highlights of our lives and the minor troubles we were encountering – though I'll never know how much she kept from me. As I grew older, left home, found new partners and settled down, we talked to each other in correspondence more openly and frankly than we did in person. Neither of us was a professional writer, though we were both teachers, and our shared love of reading meant that the written word was a strong bond between us all our lives. In my book *Why Women Read Fiction*, I describe an interview I did with my mother about her reading history, including her early secret discovery of reading via public libraries, and the way she shared novels with me over the years until I began to recommend books to her. One of them was *Gone with the Wind*, a favourite that my father gave her in 1939 on army leave, which she urged onto me, and reread as Eric was dying, to help give her Scarlett O'Hara's courage and strength. It's no coincidence that in my forties I realised I had to write a book about it, informed by research into southern history and literature, but motivated emotionally by a desire to explain its lasting appeal for women like her. She loved my *Scarlett's Women: Gone With the Wind and Its Female Fans*, and was overwhelmed by the fact I briefly discussed her in the book.

In the 1990s (alas, it's undated), she typed and dedicated to me a sixteen-page 'Autobiography of a Lancashire Girl' that gave a moving insight into her own childhood, which was so much less privileged than my own. It describes a relatively poor family in Bolton, with an irascible authoritarian father who forbade everything from her reading *School Friend* magazine to talking to boys, and refused to let her stay at school after matriculation. She discusses the sheer joy of receiving two gifts – a bound prayerbook and a bottle of lavender water (which she loved but never opened) – and the delight of camping in Staithes with the Girl Guides. Leaving school to work in a tannery, she travelled there by a smelly, dirty steam train and was assailed by the factory's foul odours. Desperate to escape, she took typing and shorthand lessons at night and moved into a solicitor's office, where she was treated well by 'delightful gentlemen' partners (one of whom committed suicide in the office so the staff were given the day off).

All her anecdotes emphasise her capacity to derive joy from solitary walking, male admiration, learning new skills, and – always – reading. I understood that, by dedicating her writing to me, she wanted me to appreciate her as a woman of considerable intelligence, frustrated by poverty and a lack of the educational and employment opportunities she so desired – and also, through her stories about boyfriends, as a woman of sexual attractiveness and desire. Alluding to the different paths she and her best friend took after school (unlike Ida, Winnie went into the sixth form, then to Cheltenham Training College, and became a teacher), she wrote, 'Money decides everything.'

All through our lives, she urged my brothers and me to take every opportunity to earn enough money to enjoy the good life she felt she never achieved. Because of a lifetime of constant money worries, she never quite understood that being wealthy isn't the only solution to life's problems.

A Tale of Two Wedding Photographs

Six months before my mother died, DJ and I got married for practical reasons, after three decades of cohabitation. Alas, she was too ill to attend the wedding, though I showed her at the residential home the video my niece made of it, and took her cake and photos. She was touched that, bouquet-less, I carried in my hand one of the flowers she had sent me. A month later, she wrote in her notebook an article she called 'A Tale of Two Photographs'. It begins with a description of two photos she had on the wall of her tiny bedroom: one in sepia of her wedding, 4 October 1941; the other in colour of my wedding, 29 August 2003.

Eric was on leave from a posting in Northern Ireland. He spent his 21st birthday on Dunkirk Beach and on his return was posted to a O.C.T.U. [Officer Cadet Training Unit] and then to Belfast. I was a typist working for Philip Rennison, the Town Clerk of Bolton, earning 12/6d per week. I knew nothing of university education and, having achieved Matriculation, thought I was well educated and equipped for the world. How wrong and ignorant I was, and would remain so for the rest of my life.

The reception, at a nice hotel in Bradshawgate, had a limited number of guests because of wartime restrictions (for financial reasons, much to her parents' relief), and afterwards they went along to a photographer's studio to have the wedding photograph taken. She contrasted this with my wedding:

> The bridegroom was a retired University Dean, an academic who knew all about education. As did the bride, my dearly loved daughter. Her life had taken place down a corridor of universities . . . and now she is a Professor and Head of the School of English at Exeter University. And she earns more than 12/6d a week, and is educated and well-equipped for life!

She expressed regret that her wedding photograph wasn't in colour, as her outfit was 'a lovely shade of blue, my hat maroon, my bouquet sweet peas. This was the first professional outfit of my life and it was very smart and becoming. It cost just under £8 and with Eric in immaculate officer's uniform, we looked and felt proud and happy. I don't think I ever wore the outfit again . . . No, my uniform very soon became pinny and rubber gloves.' By contrast, she called my wedding outfit bought in Milan during our pre-wedding holiday a 'flamingo dress' in 'exquisite fabric and delicate colours'. 'Now *she* will wear it many times, I hope, in the luxurious homes of rich people and in the Halls and corridors of higher education. Not a pinny in sight!' Ah, if only higher education removed the need for a pinny . . .

Their honeymoon, with my father on leave, was a few days in the Old England Hotel, Windermere, driving in Eric's father's loaned Armstrong Siddeley on a few illegal gallons of rationed petrol donated by the chief constable she knew through work. 'It never stopped raining – everywhere was sodden – so not a marvellous start for us – signs of things to come. Not a "happy ever after."' She contrasted this with our little honeymoon, after a glorious summer, driving our own car 'filled with legally acquired petrol', to stay in a flat belonging to two friends overlooking Cornwall's Polperro harbour, often in sunshine. 'So, let us hope, a sign of things to come.'

These accounts are full of self-deprecation, sadness and a certain bitterness. My mother was leaving me a legacy of her pride and pleasure in the life I had been able to live. Education for her was a supreme gift and privilege, and in these contrasting portraits she saw the different lives our class, gender and educational positions had delivered. For her, marriage and children took away freedoms to explore, experiment, and build a satisfying working life. She undoubtedly envied as well as admired me, and rereading her writings I now understand more profoundly how the differences in our lives created a lifelong tension between us. As a mother, she wanted me to escape drudgery and unhappiness, and her solution was to avoid having children. But as a woman she felt both impatient and angry that I was living a life so different from hers that we sometimes found it hard to comprehend and tolerate each other.

My Second Mother

On 7 September 1969, my mother wrote a letter to Louise, the woman who'd taken me in when I first arrived in New York. Naively, I'd assumed I could spend my first ten days in the US hanging out with people in Manhattan (I hadn't reckoned on the sheer expense of the city), and as backup I had one phone number to call – that of Louise, a friend of a friend. I stayed in her studio apartment, sleeping on the floor, for ten days before flying South. Ida wrote a lovely letter to her telling her how 'unnerving it was for us to see a daughter off on such an adventure'. She was thankful that that daughter was able to depend on 'some unknown Guardian Angel in New York to help her'.

This guardian angel was rather racier than my mother imagined. She was a Jewish woman with a fascinating past as a young trade union organiser in New York's Garment District, a job she gave up for marriage and motherhood. She then lived a conventional and rather stifling married life in suburban Queens, and at the age of forty-seven left her husband and rented an apartment in the heart of Manhattan. She had a long-term married lover who was never going to leave his wife and behaved very badly towards Louise. Meanwhile she was experimenting with new freedoms – jobs, friends and lovers – and was looking for a playmate.

In those ten days, when my mother thought we were going round art galleries and window-shopping along Fifth Avenue, Louise took me to jazz clubs and bars where she was hoping to pick up men. At the Goose and Gherkin, towards the end of my first week, we were chatted up by two friends of similar ages to our own: Frank, a married Catholic man in his fifties with ten children, and Paul, a thirty-five-year-old single man. About to move on to Baton Rouge, I had no interest in starting a new relationship, but Louise did – and she and Frank fell passionately in love and began a doomed affair that lasted well beyond my visit, ending only when Louise found another lover. When I left for Louisiana, I promised to write – and we exchanged regular letters in the way I always had with my first mother. Despite the twenty years between our ages, we shared ideas about our emotional lives, and I sympathised with her complicated relationship with her sons, Larry and Martin. I chided her in these letters for referring to her 'old age', saying she 'behaves and looks like a 22-year-old'. I said how good it was to be able to discuss romantic and sexual feelings with her, as she always came up with 'shrewd observations and spot-on advice'. Unlike Ida and me, we shared a progressive politics.

A Surrogate Daughter

When I returned to New York the following summer, and as I was making reckless plans to throw my degree overboard and stay in New York with Perry, she offered 'wise and sensible' advice (I presume urging caution about burning my boats). I commented that it was a pity she'd never had a daughter – 'she'd have been a very lucky person'. Louise's younger son was exactly my age, and he had distanced himself from her and his father by becoming the punk musician 'Martin Rev' and living in considerable poverty with a woman who had several children of her own. There's no doubt that Louise began to think of me as a surrogate daughter, and she treated me as such until her death. For my part, when living in the States, I treated her like the liberal and permissive mother of my dreams. I confided in her about my cultural and political anxieties, my distaste for southern racism and conservatism, and an increasingly complicated emotional life in a place where women were supposed to be southern belles and double standards applied to sexual behaviour. I felt I'd gone back decades, and compared with London in the 1960s indeed I had. As a sophisticated New Yorker who despised and never wished to visit the Deep South, Louise understood only too well; at the time Ida didn't know enough about US history to be able to imagine my experience of that region.

My brief sojourn to the West Coast to stay with Shelley Winters occupied many a letter to Louise during the summer of 1970. To her, rather than to Ida, I described the Hollywood scene with all its excess, glamour and decadence. The alcoholic hangers-on to Shelley, the chaotic but buzzy household, and Perry's actor-ly self-centeredness all featured in my letters, and I confided in her about my doubts relating to this very new relationship. In December, when Perry and I split up, I wrote in some detail about why it had failed, and how sad it made me. I couldn't really admit to my shrewd mother – who had known all along the relationship was doomed – the ambivalence I had always felt about him. Louise confided in me about her fraught yearning for her wayward married lover ('you are the most highly romantic/sensual woman I know', I rather extravagantly told her), and her decision not to return to her husband to 'make a dead marriage work again'. I admitted to her that I'd been chided by the English department secretary for turning up to teach 'without proper foundations' (i.e. bra-less), and I described the 'drab men' at the university after a summer among showbiz folk.

I was fast becoming known on campus as 'a dangerous foreign radical' because of my fiery speeches and articles in the college newspaper about Women's Liberation: 'Last year I was "British Girl on campus", this year "The Libbie".' One professor told me that senior faculty resented me for not simply acting like a graduate student; I told Louise that hostility had come to a head at a party when a professor cornered me in his yard and was about to hit me, until his wife turned up and angrily rebuked him. I kept such details from my birth mother but described all of it to Louise, who shared Ida's alarm at the dizzying changes taking place in me as a result of my uncompromising feminism. In a letter around that time, I told her that my brother and my cousin had each got engaged, and I was 'the only fancy-free one left out of my whole family, cousins included'. I admitted to a loneliness that was hard to bear, tempered somewhat by the accounts of miserable marriages from other women on the 'sensitivity retreat', and from Louise herself.

Sexual Experiments

When I returned to England and became involved with a recently separated man with three children, I wrote to Louise admitting to my mother's deep horror and disgust. Ida had called me 'wicked', and this caused a considerable breach between us. Louise, who had form in such relationships, was currently involved with a new married man; she empathised with my dilemma and offered no judgement. On the contrary, she shared with me her joy in a glorious sexual affair and her reluctance to force things in case of pushing him away altogether. I responded by saying that I was achieving an emotional distance from my mother, which was enabling me to cope with life and feel more independent. This wasn't true, as my early twenties were full of turmoil, messy relationships, and involvements with separated fathers whose children I simply couldn't handle.

Out of mingled shame and defiance, I was unable to engage with my mother's wisdom and appalled concern for my reckless involvement with such men. My alternative mother Louise's similar follies and her support seemed more appealing. I wrote that I felt 'in a sea of no-rules and no-barriers – one of my friends says women like me are trailblazers moulding their own patterns and creating their own lives, because there are no models and examples to emulate'. This was a narcissistic interpretation of the emotional messes I was getting into, as my feminist wilful blindness led me to misread other people's needs and dilemmas. For instance, I encouraged a woman to go for an abortion it turned out she didn't really want, and I admitted to 'terrible jealousy' of my partner's children, on whom (understandably during divorce negotiations) he lavished attention. I pronounced those children 'fairly difficult ... with their silly jokes and constant demands', though I acknowledged I seemed to be becoming a 'sour old maid'.

When that relationship folded, I told Louise my mother had written to say, 'Well, you may cry yourself to sleep every night, but many women are doing just that, with a man beside them.' I was glad my break-up was sharp and swift, since I knew Louise had suffered 'the cruellest, the long, slow, drawn-out kind'. I told her that every woman I knew was 'breeding like mad'– even those who vowed they weren't interested – and I was feeling sad and lonely because this placed a barrier between childless people and their friends 'who've entered the whole scene of sleepless nights, breast-feeding and early bedtimes'. Unlike my first mother, my second couldn't understand my reluctance to have children. A devoted mother and step-grandmother who chided her older son for his childlessness, Louise often told me – to my annoyance – what a good mother I would be.

Distancing from my Second Mother

My next love affair, which has lasted to this day, was with DJ – who appeared at the time to have no children (see Chapter 1). We were both free spirits, and in the early days there was much flouncing out and threats of parting. While I maintained in my correspondence with Ida that all was well (and this time I'd found an unmarried childfree partner!), I wrote to Louise about our 'sharply differing needs and desires' in a relationship 'with no economic reasons or children to force you to patch up differences – we're free as air to say goodbye and have to make the choice to be together every day'.

I kept urging her to come to stay with us – which she did with increasing frequency – until one summer, after a hysterectomy, she insisted on coming to the UK for three weeks and was in a bad physical and emotional state.

It was a very long three weeks in a small house. While she expected to be cosseted and entertained, I was trying to finish writing my DPhil thesis alongside a full-time teaching job, something she couldn't understand. I realised she too was seeking a mother to cherish and comfort her. That summer I finally weaned myself off this second mother, and became resentful of her lack of comprehension of my working life and her petulant demands on my time. By contrast, and with hindsight, I realise how little my independent mother demanded of me – even if she occasionally expressed some jealousy that Louise was staying with us yet again, and so was invited less frequently. The fact that Louise and I had been buddies and confidantes about our colourful sexual lives meant we had bonded over our mutual insecurities and self-hatred. This started to irk me as I realised how destructive it had become to us both.

As I got older, more professionally established and more secure in my relationship with DJ, I no longer needed Louise's reassurances or advice, and as with Ida, I moved to distance myself in order to avoid her obsession with her love life and her scrutiny of mine. In 1997, I declined to meet her on her visit to England because of Ida's frailties and broken wrist after a second fall, which required my regular visits. During the next few years I gently explained that I needed all my spare time and energy to care for Ida, and although I continued to write and phone, it was a huge relief when illness and old age prevented Louise from travelling to the UK.

• • •

I learned a lot about mothering from these two mothers – not to mention others along the way. My correspondence with Ida and Louise demonstrates the different kinds of support I sought – and how much I needed their confirmation that I was living an exceptional life, beyond the norms of conventional femininity. For many feminists of my generation, ploughing a new furrow of sexual freedom and personal independence was lonely and fraught with danger, and I relied on my two mothers, as well as my female friends, to validate me. Reading my letters decades later, I am overcome with a sense of how difficult it was to nurture a child who then grew away from or beyond you, especially if that child became an adult you often found intellectually and emotionally incomprehensible and alienating. I felt trapped by and impatient with both women, but at the same time I realise they were doing their best, loving me in their own ways and sharing their wisdom and experience – even when I was unable to give them the benefit of the doubt. In later life, I understood the ways I had hurt and driven away my first mother, and the sorrow my second mother must have felt that increasingly I wasn't her playmate surrogate daughter.

As Isabel Allende suggests, living the life my mother(s) could not came at a cost. I fear I could never have offered the selfless and magnanimous love to a child that these two women showed me. Observing my friends' struggles as mothers and grandmothers, I pay homage to the self-effacing magnificence of mothers, who have to be ready at all times to give, give and – perhaps especially – forgive.

Chapter 7

Non-Biological Mothers

Living in a twenty-first-century patriarchal society, in which mothers are idealised and sentimentalised but also taken for granted and disregarded, it's hard to see where – outside religious organisations, artworks and literature – our society's role models of motherhood and family are located. With the royal family, perhaps? In 2022, the British nation was treated to two bank holidays to celebrate the Platinum Jubilee of Queen Elizabeth II – described euphorically by the *Sunday Times* as 'the world's grandmother'. This diminutive national figure, mother of four and grandma/great-grandma to many, always immaculately dressed and carrying a boxy handbag, was invested with a quasi-spiritual significance and received huge public veneration. Her death later that year was received with overwhelming public grief and outpourings of hagiographical adoration from the media. Even the cynical *Guardian* journalist, John Crace, described the late Queen as 'the nation's matriarch. The ultimate mother figure. Someone who had been an unconscious psychological support for so many people. A tabula rasa on whom they could pin their own hopes and fears.'[1]

Like many other women of my generation, I was fascinated from childhood with this Mother of the Nation. Along with other families, in 1953 my parents bought our first (tiny black-and-white) television in order to see the coronation. Despite the longueurs of the ceremony, I sensed this was a significant historical moment in British life – a new 'Elizabethan Age', led by a young and attractive woman with a handsome husband who had to walk a few steps behind. In the grey days of the 1950s and early 1960s, when most public figures we saw on TV and in newspaper photographs were besuited middle-aged or older men in drab offices, I was not alone in being mesmerised by Elizabeth and those other royal women, with their gorgeous well-cut clothes, hats, jewels and palaces.

As a child, I spent hours making scrapbooks of newspaper cuttings about the Queen and Princesses Margaret and Anne, watching eagerly the early Pathé News coverage of their activities. I remember standing with my mother and younger brother Richard in the rain for hours in our then home town, Newcastle-under-Lyme, to catch a thrilling glimpse of the Queen as she rode by in a huge Bentley. Sometimes I wished she were my mother, and I sat crammed into our tiny family car, waving at people as if I were a royal princess. The dynastic nature of the royals, led by female figures such as the Queen Mother (note her maternal title) and the Queen herself, gave us all an aspirational version of womanhood and family life through the lens of a family best known for its matriarchs.

As I grew older and more inclined to republicanism, I followed the trail of adulteries, broken marriages, the death of Diana, images of motherless princes, various sex and financial scandals involving the Queen's children, and finally the marriage of Prince Harry to a biracial American woman with whom he rejected the 'institution' and fled to America. For all their wealth, privilege and multiple homes, the royal family increasingly seemed a toxic bunch – full of division, conflict, malfunction. Rather like other families, except they had to stay closely together in order to perpetuate the myth and succession of monarchy. What kind of role model as a mother was this much-admired Queen, and how did her motherhood sit with her role as monarch? We know that she employed nannies and cooks to care for her children's daily needs, and went on long foreign tours leaving those children behind; then – reunited after months apart – formally shook their hands. In informal film and photographs, we saw this Mother/Grandmother of the Nation curled up with her many corgi dogs, or embracing passionately one of her horses. Rarely was she photographed cuddling children or grandchildren. Only in recent years has this somewhat remote and cold example of royal motherhood been challenged.

Since Diana married Prince Charles, and especially after her death, there was a softening of royal maternal images. When doting mother Diana made it clear she wouldn't go on an overseas tour without her new baby, and the Duke and Duchess of Cambridge put their three young children forward at the Platinum Jubilee celebrations, the Commonwealth Games and King Charles's coronation, there seemed to be a domestication and feminisation of the royals. In the Jubilee television comic sketch with Paddington Bear, the Queen's handbag – holding a marmalade sandwich – epitomised the way Elizabeth had become a mumsy maternal figure towards the end of her reign. Prince Charles's tribute speech even referred to 'Mummy'. The magazine *Woman and Home* answered the question many women asked: 'What does she carry in her Launer London handbag?' (The answer was reading glasses, lipstick, mirror and mints.) Cleverly, then, the Queen managed to look both maternal and non-maternal, appealing to women as mothers and non-mothers, stay-at-home and 'career women' alike. Stephen Frears's highly successful TV series *The Queen* bolstered this image.

For over seventy years, Britons were ruled by, and thus had to pay obeisance to, a woman who – despite her aristocratic lifestyle – seemed to look and behave like our mothers and grandmothers. And however glamorous the appurtenances of the royals, they are a reminder that the notion of 'family' is never simple, since behind the unifying formal group photographs there is much discord, providing fodder for the tabloid press. Referred to as 'The Firm', the shaky business model of a dynastic family was laid bare when three of the Queen's children (most notably her heir, Charles) divorced; and later, when Harry and Meghan opted out and then produced damning, demystifying TV and film interviews and a memoir. That carefully constructed mystique around the nation's most prominent, idealised family has been stripped away over the decades. And despite the unblemished reputation of the late Queen, it has become clear that the Mother of the Nation, like all other mothers, had considerable failings and failures.

It may be a relief to Queen Camilla that she can never replicate Elizabeth's role and – because of her much-demonised adulterous relationship – cannot become the nation's symbolic mother. In 2024, the future Queen, Prince William's wife Catherine, developed cancer and withdrew from active engagements, then participated in a somewhat saccharine film celebrating the joys of a warm, happy family life. She committed herself to improving the lives of young children, but wisely appeared to be avoiding a formal, symbolically maternal position within the nation.

Re-Defining 'Family'

The family in all its various forms has long been the key signifier for most societies. Its history, evolution, joys, problems and crises are the subject of many kinds of discourse, and it's a simple reference point for politicians of all colours to argue for policy changes and development ('hardworking families', etc.). Since the second wave women's movement and LGBTQ+ movements, the concept of the family has been under closer scrutiny than ever. Key texts by writers in the 1960s such as R. D. Laing, Kate Millett, Germaine Greer and Shulamith Firestone undermined our assumptions about the centrality of family relationships in a democratic society, and the debates have since raged on. I've discussed already the ways in which 'family' is being reassessed, by women with and without children, and how there is an expanding circle of familial and parental relationships. Friendship and non-biological groups or 'tribes' are crucial to childfree women, and – as marriages and partnerships disintegrate and new forms of parenting evolve – they are increasingly seen as the bedrock on which personal identity and security are based. Social media has transformed the way we establish communities and connect with others, and – in the age of WhatsApp and Instagram – the notion of a family behind closed doors, secure from the rest of the world, has largely disappeared.

That said, from 2020 onwards the Covid pandemic sent us all 'home' and focused our minds on domestic life and family ties. Physically locked behind our front doors, we were unable to visit the sick and dying, or spend real time with parents, children, relatives and friends. For those living with families or partners, this period placed great strains on the close contacts of 24/7 daily life. But for many people living alone and outside the 'bubbles' we were encouraged to form, this was a frightening imprisonment that changed many lives – and tragically ruined others. And while we were all confined to our immediate spaces with or without intimates, despite phones and computers, the process of lockdown highlighted the challenges and impossible demands of what is defined as 'family life'. Given the sharp rise in the number of single households – those born in 1965 are twice as likely to be childless as those born in 1945 – the emphasis of social services, the NHS and other bodies on the 'family' support required to get people through life has looked increasingly anachronistic.

During this period, artists Grayson and Philippa Perry made two Channel 4 TV series in which they created art while inviting celebrities and the general public to respond to the pandemic with thematic artworks. One of the themes I enjoyed in their Bristol exhibition was 'Family' – explained as representing 'a lot of different sorts of families. There are gay families, straight families, nuclear families, imaginary families, long lost families and constructed families.' The artworks included images by Boy George of his 'disco family', Anneka Rice's paintings of 'tribes' of a created community, Zoë Pyne's pictures of the 'instant alternative family' created in a student house, and Prabhneet Sondhi's portraits of her close family living on top of one another during lockdown. Philippa Perry argued that families 'are far more than a mum and a dad and 2.4 children. They are a man and his cat, a group of friends living together, a lesbian couple.' In her artwork she said she tried to represent 'many different types and different atmospheres of family' – a theme that ran throughout their show.[2]

The Perrys were echoing contemporary perspectives on what a family might be, something that feminists have spent much time exploring. In her ground-breaking 1976 study of motherhood, *Of Woman Born: Motherhood as Experience and Institution,* American poet and essayist Adrienne Rich rejects a false polarity of 'childless woman' and 'mother', which she sees as serving the institutions of motherhood and heterosexuality. She reminds us that a polarisation of 'Mothers or Amazons', 'matriarchal clan or guerilleres', didn't exist, since in the original clan all females, including little girls, were called 'mothers'. She quotes Evelyn Reed arguing that motherhood is a social rather than a physical function: 'Women ... were sisters to one another and mothers to all the children of the community without regard to which individual mother bore any child ... Aborigines described themselves as ... "brotherhoods" from the standpoint of the male and "motherhoods" from the standpoint of the female'. She notes that girl-children as young as six have cared for younger siblings.[3] Alas, this somewhat utopian vision rings hollow in our solipsistic age.

Failed Women, Spirit-Sisters, Mammies

Through recorded history, according to Rich, the childless woman is 'a failed woman' who has been burned as a witch, persecuted as lesbian, and refused the right to adopt children, all because she constitutes a threat to male hegemony. However, such women have been 'expected to serve their term for society as missionaries, nuns, teachers, nurses, maiden aunts' – though ironically the 'few available strong insights into the experience of women in general' have come from childless women such as Charlotte Brontë, Margaret Fuller, Emily Dickinson and Simone de Beauvoir.[4] Rich even suggests that many great mothers have been non-biological. Motherless literary character Jane Eyre is guided by women who 'protect, solace, teach, challenge, and nourish her in self-respect' – in Mary Daly's words, each a 'spirit-sister'. Most women have been mothers, Rich argues, 'in the sense of tenders and carers for the young, whether as sisters, aunts, nurses, teachers, foster-mothers, stepmothers . . . For most of us a woman provided the continuity and stability – but also the rejections and refusals – of our early lives, and it is with a woman's hands, eyes, body, voice, that we associate our primal sensations, our earliest social experience.'[5] She doesn't mention adoptive or surrogate mothers, though they too deserve to be honoured. In my book *Why Women Read Fiction*, I describe the considerable influence on girls' reading – and thus emotional and creative lives – of quasi-maternal female teachers and librarians.

Perhaps the most mythic non-biological mother is the 'Mammy' – a desexualised, supposedly childless woman of African American heritage who is one of the key surrogate mothers of myth and legend. Denied her own maternal role, she was given the care of the babies and young children of others – even suckling them – and, in affluent households where biological mothers had infrequent daily contact with young offspring, was very often loved by many as the 'real' mother. Adrienne Rich, raised in 1930s segregated Baltimore, wrote of her white and Black mothers as 'mothers and daughters to each other', while southern writer Lillian Smith called this 'one of the profound relationships of my life'.[6] Such a 'mother' features in iconic works ranging from *Uncle Tom's Cabin* (1852) to *Guess Who's Coming to Dinner* (1967) and *The Help* (2011), and in recent years this intimate relationship has received much critical and artistic attention, as well as fictional responses from African-American writers such as Toni Morrison, Gloria Naylor and Alice Walker. These women were economically and emotionally vital to the white family, and were raped and exploited both as slaves and free women – as well as being allowed little autonomous family life of their own, from slavery until the Civil Rights Movement. As a result, there is a heavy residue of anger, blame, guilt and need for reparation around the figure of 'Mammy'.

American southern literature and film abound with such figures, most notably the famous Mammy of *Gone With the Wind*, far more crucial in Scarlett O'Hara's life than her birth mother, and played in the 1939 Selznick film by Oscar-winner Hattie McDaniel. In 2001 African-American author Alice Randall published *The Wind Done Gone*, a witty parody and decidedly unromantic story about southern miscegenation in which all the Black and white characters are related and end up buried together. Toni Morrison's *Beloved* (1987) is the best example of a work that demonstrates the tragic denial of Black women's motherhood, resulting in Sethe's murder of her 'best thing' – daughter Beloved, who returns to haunt her. A later novel by white writer Damon Galgut focusing on apartheid South Africa, *The Promise*, features Salome, a 'mammy' who is promised a home by her white employers. That promise is repeatedly broken, but it becomes a key factor in the divisions in and breakdown of the white family's relations. The loyalty Salome inspires in the white mother and her daughter testifies to the racial and political importance of those non-biological ties that challenge the notion of the white family.[7]

In the UK, there is a recurrent trope in political discourse about 'the nanny state' – a phrase used to denigrate any attempt to improve people's daily lives by good advice thought to be laid on with a trowel. This phrase has alluded to dietary choices, warm clothing, smoking, vaping and other activities, and reveals popular media's contempt for a woman – like Mammy – who knows what would be good for you (the child or childlike figure), but whom you (the rebellious child) deeply resents. In recent years, I noticed that nannies, nans and grannies (the subject of many a derogatory or patronising media reference) are becoming more vocal and indeed militant as they increasingly participate in social and political life, and join demonstrations for or against climate breakdown or immigration. These women, who have long been the backbone of many families and voluntary/political organisations, should no longer be dismissed as 'sweet old dears'.

Rainbow Families

In our times, alternative families of mixed heritage and race have countered the normative white patriarchal family. Think of Madonna and her adopted children and (failed) Malawi school project, and Angelina Jolie with her multicultural adopted kids. Perhaps in a PR response to the Black Lives Matter movement, it seems that almost every British TV programme, film and advertisement features racially mixed characters and families. Long before these, however, was the outstanding example of African-American Josephine Baker – singer, radical war hero and political activist – who couldn't give birth to children herself but set out to create a 'Rainbow Tribe' of children from poor families and orphanages. Described by Margo Jefferson as a 'visionary,' Baker once said: 'Surely the day will come when color means nothing more than the skin tone, when religion is seen uniquely as a way to speak one's soul; when birth places have the weight of a throw of the dice and all men are born free, when understanding breeds love and brotherhood.'[8]

Over many years, and with considerable financial and other challenges, Baker and her husband Jo Bouillon adopted twelve children of different races and nationalities, under the French Family Code of 1939, a pro-natalist decree which offered cash and other incentives for mothers to stay at home to care for children, and to increase a declining population.[9] In 1957, she and Bouillon wrote a children's book, *The Rainbow Tribe*, and although her example wasn't widely followed, it did inspire more French people to adopt children from other countries during the 1960s.

Jefferson admires Baker primarily for her disregard of race, religion and birthplace in favour of skill and talent. She sees this as a challenge to family connections and what she says is 'so American and entitled, this fetish worship of ancestors' loss and deprivation ... Wearing the garb of ancestral suffering like it was vintage clothing.'[10] I share Jefferson's impatience with this obsession with family legacy and history, though I believe it helps explain why a choice to be childfree must be far more difficult for women of colour than for white women.

Mothering and Mother-Love

For many childless or childfree women, the obsession with legacy can be oppressive, and less restrictive concepts of motherhood or family can be liberating. My own biological family (parents and brothers) is probably fairly typical. Besides warm exchanges, longstanding friendship, shared humour and experiences, we have had deep conflicts, fractured ties, bitter exchanges, and long periods of zero communication followed by later-life reconciliation and mutual concern. By contrast, I have experienced less-fraught motherly feelings towards students, friends, neighbours and colleagues, and have compensated for my childfreeness with ties of friendship and support. Individual teachers are often acknowledged by artists and writers as key figures in their cultural and emotional development. The close attention to their needs and aspirations, and recognition of their unique qualities, are seen as positively parental – and in the case of women teachers, almost maternal. I remember a male teaching colleague being bewildered by a mature woman student running crying out of his office; he came to me and asked me to pursue and calm her as 'a woman could handle this so much better'. How many aunts, grandmothers, close women-friends and godmothers have been brought in to mediate between biological parents and fractious or rebellious children – with all the advantages of not being on the front line? Mother-love is a quality that extends beyond genetic ties.

I wonder if mother-love is always synonymous with providing and nurturing. When I think of the school runs, meals cooked, cakes baked, knees bandaged, tears wiped, clothes washed, nits treated, bedtime stories told, geraniums dead-headed, birthday and Christmas cards written . . . I feel awed by women's capacity to care, multitask and hold everything together. Pride in one's house and garden, though sometimes shared by men, is often developed and sustained by the mother of the house. During the pandemic lockdowns, it became clear that women were doing the lion's share of domestic work, home schooling and emotional labour. It would be interesting to know how many childless women sublimate their maternal instincts by enthusiastic catering – since the preparation and sharing of food is so central to all societies, even if ready-made microwaved meals have overtaken the communal dinner. A much-quoted story about cake mixes in the 1950s and early 1960s is that the instructions called for an egg to be added to the mix so that women would feel they were creating something (like a baby).

Food is spoken of as 'a love language', allowing people to offer one another physical and emotional sustenance. I am a lucky (and unusual!) woman since my partner DJ speaks this language to me daily, as he offers up magnificent meals. Feeding and nurturing a garden, or even a window box, offers women like me the opportunity to care and fuss over living plants that hopefully respond to maternal attention. But there are also the women who – with little aptitude for domestic skills – have resented the need to provide. In a gloriously comic passage of her memoir, Lorna Sage says of her mother, 'She just wished – out loud, quite often – that the housework would do itself. In the same spirit she cursed cooking and as she dumped our plates in front of us on the eating end of the table she would announce that we could take it or leave it, and that she wished we could all live on pills.'[11] These words echo those in many feminist novels and non-fiction about the tedium of daily food provision, and certainly remind me of my own mother's weariness at the endless rounds of cooking for five people in the years before instant meals and McDonald's. As DJ and our friends (mostly superb cooks) can testify, I have few culinary skills, and have always been eager to get out of the kitchen as soon as possible.

While mothers are generally seen as providers – cooking, nursing, gift-giving, domestic organisation – there are many women who provide those services for families not their own, or people who need the kind of nurturing generally associated with the maternal. So one can be a mother without having children, and can avoid the tensions and challenges of biological ties in favour of the pleasures of caring. Many girls have entered the nursing or teaching profession because they know such work will satisfy their desire to work with children. As Lucy Worsley, who is childfree, said in an interview in which she described writing novels for children, 'there are different ways of being maternal beyond just biology'.[12] And after Raymond Briggs died in August 2022, Louisa Young reported that he turned down the post of Children's Laureate and was heard on the radio saying, 'I've no interest in children. Didn't want to have any' – though he and his wife, unable to conceive, had an imaginary daughter, Chrysanthemum-Pearl. Other writers such as Enid Blyton, A. A. Milne, Dr Seuss and Maurice Sendak have expressed similar sentiments about children – though in all cases their feelings were complicated by life experiences and a need for quiet spaces to write.[13] I myself organised three children's literature festivals in Exeter and Liverpool without knowing much about children's literary tastes or indeed children's writers. That said, I recall feeling deeply moved at the sight of crowds of enthusiastic children thronging round Julia Davidson and Michael Morpurgo, whose work they knew off by heart.

In all these ways, mothering and motherhood can be seen to have multiple forms and meanings. And as young women delay or decide against having children of their own, and older people living long lives outnumber the young, non-biological mothers will need to fill the gaps with nurturing that is traditionally provided by biological mothers.

Pets – substitute children?

A familiar trope about childlessness is that pets are substitute babies. Helen Macdonald, of *H is for Hawk* fame, said that caring for baby peregrine falcons probably absorbed all her maternal instincts. Nina Jervis published a book called *I'd Rather Get a Cat and Save the Planet: Conversations with Childfree Women*. Isabel Allende wrote that she told her son, Nicolás, 'instead of bringing children into the world he could get a dog, and he has never forgiven me'. His response was to marry at twenty-two and have three children in five years. Allende's ambiguous comment: 'As for me, my grandchildren are okay, but I also love dogs.'[14]

And then there was the phenomenon of pandemic pet-ownership. During the first Covid lockdown in 2020, 3.2 million Britons acquired a pet – mainly cats and dogs. Everywhere I went – shops, cafés and friends' homes – I almost tripped over a cute new puppy; and on Zoom, Facebook and Twitter there were videos and photos of adorable kittens causing mayhem. It seemed that young couples, recently bonded, saw this as their first, safe foray into family life without the more serious commitment to, and hassle of, babies. Older childless couples also saw this as a way of becoming late parents at a very lonely time. In October 2021, journalist Pilita Clark reported that, as offices reopened in the US, the 'separation anxiety' workers felt about returning to work without their pets had led them to request employers to allow pets in the office. Furthermore, the Pets at Home care business was offering its employees 'PETernity leave' – a day off to settle in a new pet – and a British firm Boxpark posted a social media poll asking what people thought of an employee who had asked for paternity leave to look after a new puppy.[15] In 2023, UK shoppers spent £873 million on Christmas presents for their dogs and cats, while 37 per cent of dog lovers have appointed dog-parents and/or added details of dog care in their wills.[16] Alas, and predictably, once employees had to return to work, and the cost-of-living crisis hit the country, many pets were abandoned or taken to animal rescue centres.

In 2022, French presidential candidate Marine Le Pen sought to woo voters by presenting herself as a cat-lover and cat breeder. A woman soft on her cats was seen as a vote-winner, and who knows how many voters (perhaps especially women) fell for this? *Woman and Home* reported that the Queen's corgis were fed luxury meals from silver bowls and flown in private jets from Balmoral Castle to Windsor.[17] I am struck by the number of references on Twitter/X to people's pets, something that in previous decades would have been regarded as embarrassingly revealing. I checked one day in April 2022, when dogs were the main subject, and there were multiple references to 'our boy', 'our lovely rescue dog', '[an adopted dog] a life saver … Can't explain how much we all love her'; one claimed the Dogs of Twitter 'play a significant part in keeping me sane'. Dogs of Twitter and Cats of Twitter provide photos, videos, birthday announcements, witty commentaries on, eulogies to and requests for advice about precious pets. The term 'cat' is the most searched for on the internet, and remains the most popular category; a figure of 26 billion views is often cited, with dogs not far behind. The top stars, Japanese cat Motimaru and Siberian husky Mishka, are said to have received almost 100 million views between them. But although some authors thank their pets for helping them through the difficult process of creation, and pet owners spend more and more on complex surgery and medications, we haven't yet got to the point where obituaries describe the deceased as 'survived by' a dog or cat, even though in many cases this creature is valued as highly as the human members of the 'family'.

The Pope's Anxieties

The growing fashion for pet ownership is causing moral and political anxiety, in light of the 'demographic winter' of dramatically reduced global birth rates. Pope Francis has even intervened in the debate. Using that familiar term applied to the childfree, he talked of choosing pets over children as a 'form of selfishness'. In his view, pet-keeping is 'a denial of fatherhood and motherhood and diminishes us, takes away our humanity'. As a result, 'civilisation grows old without humanity because we lose the richness of fatherhood and motherhood, and it is the country that suffers'.[18] He is not alone in expressing concern about the birth rate, or relating it to the general health (or growth of population) of a nation. As the world's leading Catholic, he is understandably alarmed that people are voting with their feet, using the contraception and abortion he condemns. He feels no empathy with those who adopt a lifestyle that is more conducive to democratic personal relationships and playful inter-species parenting, with men and women hedging their bets about the future of the planet and thus the human race. Perhaps he might consider the ordination of married male and female priests who could supply the 'richness of fatherhood and motherhood' he feels civilisation requires.

Journalist Simon Kelner took issue with the Pope. Far from 'selfishness', Kelner argues that pet-keeping helps us to understand 'how to be more selfless, caring and responsible ... We get lessons in unconditional love, and loyalty ... We learn how to live in the present by appreciating the pleasure of small things, like the wag of a tail, or an impromptu purr.' Unashamedly admitting he describes himself as his dog's father, and engages in 'conversations', he suggests that owning a pet teaches us about life, love and loss, and how to grieve – improving us as people.[19]

Mothering Cats

For people living alone, and those not ready or unable to have children (or with children living a long distance away), having a companion animal can make all the difference to their daily life and mental health, so it's not surprising many older childless women (including a generation of LGBTQ+ people for whom parenthood wasn't possible) have dogs or cats.

Tania, a poet I quoted earlier who is certain she will always live alone, has written lyrically about her relationship with cats:

> My cats have been the creatures I have felt the closest to in my life. My cat, Zac, was my companion for 16 years, he made me feel more cared for and understood than any human has, and the grief when he died was enormous. And my cat now, Sylvie, is my favourite creature in the world. I wouldn't be as happy living the way I do without her, she is wonderful company.

Mind you, Tania is well aware of the stereotype: 'I have been feeling recently that I would have been the woman living with her cat on the edge of the village that people would have called a witch and tried to burn!' She has decided to 'embrace that identity fully'.

The early modern European superstition lingers that a woman living alone with a cat has magical or demonic powers, a trope repeated in fairy tales and literature. Cats are sensual and intuitive creatures that cannot be bidden. The association with witchcraft, given a modern spin with the 'crazy cat lady' stereotype, seems to derive from a fear of that special relationship women have established with felines. Artists from Gwen John and Barbara Hepworth to Tracey Emin have paid tribute to their cats. In her memoir *The Year of the Cat: A Love Story* (2023), journalist Rhiannon Lucy Cosslett embraces the notion of the cat lady to explore the way her kitten Mackerel helped her healing process after severe PTSD. She wonders how many 'crazy cat ladies' have been, as she was, victims of male violence, suggesting such women may have lost faith in human beings and instead identify with stray, wounded animals. Donald Trump's vice president, J. D. Vance, would undoubtedly feel it confirmed his view of a type of woman who has no stake in her country's future.

Doris Lessing's unsentimental paean to cats, *Particularly Cats* (1967), made a strong impression on me and I've been drawn to cats ever since. Though coming from a pet-free family, along with many other childfree women I've found myself intrigued by these mysterious creatures. As soon as I settled into my home in Bristol in the early 1970s, I was given an unusual female tortoiseshell with six toes. For two decades my ex- and current partners and I cared for her, as well as one of her kittens we decided to keep. Many other childless cat-owning friends shared stories, anxieties and joys, and we were drawn into a community concerned about worming, special diets and kidney failure. After their deaths, I mourned them and never got another, mainly because I live on a busy road that has killed many of my neighbours' cats. 'Empty nest syndrome' in relation to children has been the subject of many a novel and film, and I certainly experienced it myself, often believing I saw one or other of my cats around corners or near the place we put their bowls. Caring for them, I learned a lot about – and was able to empathise with – human mother-love. One big advantage of cats over children is that they rarely leave home, unless lost or killed. The nest is empty only when their lives are ended; they don't go on to marry someone you don't like, fall out with you irrevocably, or make a mess of their lives that you have to sort out. The lack of complexity in a relationship with pets is one of its attractions – that is, until pet owners realise animals have personality and physical problems of their own, and that vet bills may well cost an arm and a leg.

What pet ownership gives people – those with as well as without children – is the opportunity to be a different kind of parent, one involved in the fascinating interspecies communication between human and beast. You can't reason or have an adult conversation with a dog or cat, but you can experiment with ways of parenting, talking without words, and experiencing the joy of cuddling a creature that will love or tolerate you without judgement or criticism. The pet-care site Rover.com suggests that getting a dog is a greater commitment for a couple than opening a joint bank account, and is the best preparation for a baby. (Perhaps would-be mothers should avoid the 2024 film *Nightbitch* based on Rachel Yoder's magic-realist novel, which imagines a frustrated and overworked at-home mother transformed into a wild, scruffy dog.) Since increasingly – for economic, social and personal reasons – women choose not to reproduce, we acquire pets to satisfy our maternal urges and fill our homes with creatures that give us the chance to provide love, concern and little treats. These relationships also allow play-parenting in a world of climate emergency, nuclear threat and economic instability, all of which make many of us sceptical about a secure and hopeful future for any children we might have. No wonder the Pope is concerned.

Conclusion
Childless by Choice –
What does it Mean?

In early 2023, after a relaxing holiday in Tenerife, I contracted Covid and spent the best part of a week in bed, sleeping and unable to function. Despite recovering physically, I fell into a deep depression caused by the virus and exacerbated by profound fatigue, and ended up getting antidepressants prescribed by my GP. For much of that year, instead of planning ahead, I found myself experiencing feelings typical of people my age: nostalgia for the vitality of youth; looking back sadly to roads not taken; regrets about past decisions and actions; loss of self-belief; a fear of inevitable physical and mental decline; and a sense of the sheer pointlessness of life in my final years. But there was another theme running through my depression: a regret that I didn't have energetic young people around me regularly to offer hope and optimism for the future.

While I was ill and depressed, I came across a short book by Sophie Lewis and thought this might be the answer to my dilemma about being childless/free. *Abolish the Family* is

'A Manifesto for Care and Liberation', an apocalyptic vision of the family – the basic unit of capitalism. She argues the family privatises care and thus has a history of perpetual crisis, since this is the site of most of our society's rapes and murders, bullying, manipulation and sexual assault. Lewis quotes Betty Friedan in 1963 describing the private home as 'a comfortable concentration camp'. She advocates the old duo of 'kith and kin', with kith suggesting relations between people on the grounds of 'knowledge, practice, and place, rather than race, descent, and identity'. She is inspired by philosopher Donna Haraway's rejection of ties through blood, advocating instead 'models of solidarity and human unity and difference rooted in friendship, work, partially shared purposes, intractable collective pain, inescapable mortality, and persistent hope'. The book ends with Lewis saying she doesn't know what will follow the family, which will be after her day. Approvingly, she quotes feminist sociologists Michèle Barrett and Mary McIntosh – who, when asked what they would put in place of the family, said 'nothing'.[1]

This is all intellectually coherent, but where does it leave us? Lewis offers no feasible alternative, and when I think back on all the failed attempts of western societies to establish new forms of living outside or beyond the family, I feel sceptical of utopian visions of social organisation. Let's face it, the bonds of kinship – the 'chain of life' as archaeologist Alice Roberts calls it – are all too precious. In recent times, we've been reminded of this as Ukraine and Gaza exploded, with families brutally torn apart. Surely families are where children should be safe, and the sight of Ukrainian and Palestinian child orphans, and aged and disabled people in hospitals or temporary shelters, reminds us that – if for nothing else – this institution exists to protect and cherish the vulnerable and needy. It's thus hard to see what could replace it. How many people can I, as a free detached individual, be expected to care about and look after? Ideally all my fellow citizens, but realistically only those who are closely related to me or linked by long friendship. That was the lesson I learned when my younger friends had their children and excluded or failed to include me in their care. Let's face it, nurturing kids requires close and continual attention to their characters and needs, and unless you are the parent in daily contact with them, you will probably misread signals, seem tone-deaf, and get things wrong. That's one reason communes tend to fail, as adults who are either without children or awkward around them are easily distracted, bored or absent.

When you fall ill, you want familiar faces and bodies around you, and while DJ – some years older than me – has always been here, he had Covid alongside me, and has various physical challenges that preoccupy him. As I've said, we both have cousins, nieces and nephews, but only one of them lives or works near us – and, to be honest, with busy lives none of us has made huge efforts to keep in touch, despite the fact we always enjoy one another's company when we meet at weddings, birthdays and (increasingly) funerals. During that post-Covid time, I fantasised – if DJ weren't around – about a devoted adult daughter or son who would come running to my bedside, give me a hug and organise food shopping, cooking and washing. I realise that my life and health are significant to many relatives, friends and neighbours, and they would come to my aid if asked – though my brothers and some of my closest friends live a long way away and are usually accessible only by WhatsApp, FaceTime or email. But surely, I thought to myself, since a lifetime's physical intimacy and familiarity between parents and children can rarely be matched by siblings and friends, any child I had would jump to it if I asked them to come and care for me.

These were the self-pitying and mournful thoughts that exacerbated my depression.

So whom was I kidding? Chances are I wouldn't be living anywhere near my child(ren), and they would have jobs, partners, children, problems and preoccupations that would prevent close involvement with an aged mother. We may well have fallen out years before my dotage, and/or their partners might resent any demands I made for time and support. I cheer myself with the thought that, since I don't have to be the 'bank of mum and dad', I should have sufficient resources to pay for professional nursing care in my final years. Although this may involve leaving my comfortable house and moving to a small flat, a residential or care home, I know that – however lonely – I will be relying on the kindness of strangers and won't be a burden on my 'family'. As I comfort myself with that thought, I also consider how grim it must be for some people to be alone – loneliness is now seen as a major global problem, especially among the elderly – and to know they can't afford to pay for care and they have no one around willing to provide it. A chilling report in September 2024 noted a dramatic rise in funerals or cremations arranged and paid for by the UK's local councils, because there was no one close to the deceased to organise or fund them.

In the last year or so, as friends and family members in their seventies and eighties have become ill or died, surrounded or strongly supported by their children and grandchildren, I've felt envy and suppressed resentment that this won't happen to me. Throughout my life, I've developed considerable self-sufficiency, which I hope will carry me through illness and infirmity, but there is a sterile feeling about this which reminds me of a cold hospital ward as opposed to a warm family bedroom. Thinking back to my ex-colleague Avril's suicide, like her I ask myself who I am living for, and what purpose does my life have now I'm no longer economically active and have no offspring or grandchildren? Despite my various post-career activities, I feel somewhat isolated by reminders of family bonds, which I can see becoming ever more important as people age. My brothers, sister- and brother-in-law all have children who keep in regular touch, enjoy convivial gatherings, and respond to health and other crises (and of course request financial help from time to time). My oldest friends are called on to help out with their grandchildren while parents recover from illness or need some respite; two women close to me have become delighted great-grandmothers. There are even 'grantenatal classes' to teach rusty grandparents how to look after their children's babies. When my cousin Laurence was terminally ill, his four children and many grandchildren visited regularly, and when one granddaughter, Rachel, told him she was thinking about him, he replied with a beatific smile, 'I think about you all, all the time.' His peaceful death was described to me in that well-worn phrase, 'surrounded by his loving family'. When families call on you, you have to respond, and of course that makes you feel needed and loved. These are the bonds I described earlier; they can't be magicked out of nowhere, and they rely on longevity and regular communication.

Age and experience often bring changes that mellow people. While the media obsessed about the bitter silence between Princes William and Harry or Noel and Liam Gallagher, in 2024 the Gallagher brothers announced they were to halt that long feud and tour again as the group Oasis. The angry feelings of more than a decade had softened into a creative (financially lucrative!) compromise, and possibly an emotional reconciliation. Similarly, after years of painful estrangement, tempered only by occasional meetings, my relationship with my younger brother Richard and his wife Lynda was rekindled when they came to our later-years wedding, got together after my parents' deaths, invited us to their sons' weddings, and offered us a holiday in their Mallorca flat after we visited them in London. Lynda was very ill, and the visit therefore had a poignant and tender tone (partly because we avoided political discussion, a cause of great conflict in the past). It was a regretful reminder of the ties we had lost over the years, especially with our nephews Oliver and Alex and their children, and it revived a relationship that has blossomed ever since and will be even more important now Lynda has died. And in the last year, two young women

– my second cousin and my ex-partner's daughter – came to live in Bristol and we established an ongoing friendship with them. These familial connections have given me much pleasure, soothing my worries about the growing vulnerability of age with the hope of support from longstanding family members to whom one has to prove nothing, and the fillip of embracing new young people in my life. I now understand why childless writer Simone de Beauvoir 'adopted' an adult woman as a daughter in her late life.

In the course of writing this book, I've had many – often extremely emotional – conversations with friends and acquaintances (though not with my brothers and their children – a bit too close to the bone). I thought I was fairly unusual in feeling ambivalent about my own choice, but every time I raise the subject with parents, I find many of them have had conflicted feelings about bearing and caring for their children, and thus some jealousy of my childfree state. The veil of silence that once covered some people's ambivalence or hostility towards their own children, and regrets about having a family at all, has been removed by brave journalists and writers who expose the difficult challenges of being a parent in a complicated world that gives them little support. In extreme cases, women have given up mothering altogether. *The Abandoners* (2024) is writer Begoña Gómez Ursaiz's account of immigrant mothers, as well as famous artistic women (e.g. Muriel Spark, Ingrid Bergman, Joni Mitchell) leaving their children, in order to save their own and those children's lives and sanity. (Joni Mitchell later successfully reconnected with her daughter.) The poet Rosie Jackson, who left her son behind with his father to develop her career and find herself, published *Women Who Leave* (1994) about creative women who had done this (Doris Lessing, Frieda Lawrence, Yoko Ono, et al.), followed by a memoir, *The Glass Mother* (2016), about her own decision.

What a complex and emotive subject this is – demonstrated by the weight of discussion in the press and online about the desirability of choosing to parent. Newspapers and radio programmes regularly feature women, or occasionally couples, usually in their late twenties or thirties, in the midst of a dilemma about whether to go ahead. This is accompanied by distressing accounts of involuntary childlessness, baby loss, failed IVF treatments, surrogacy problems, and anguished couples eager to reduce their carbon footprint by refusing to reproduce. Then there are young writers complaining that people dislike them for being 'DINKS' (dual income, no kids) when all they want is a comfy life without the financial burdens inherent in childbearing. Although a global problem, in the UK alone the cost of living and a lack of affordable housing have forced would-be parents to delay fertility treatment, or give up the idea of having a child altogether.[2] The Pregnant Then Screwed charity claims that nearly one-fifth of parents (mostly women) have been forced to leave work because of expensive childcare. Given the fact we still don't have equal pay and opportunities for women, it's usually the mother who steps back into the role of unpaid carer, and she rarely resumes her pre-children career trajectory.

How can a woman make a free and considered choice to have a baby when there are so many economic, social and political pressures and barriers in the way? However sentimental politicians and commentators are about motherhood, and, aside from prohibitively expensive private childcare and some enlightened workplaces, there is little government help and few civic amenities enabling women to participate in or return to the workplace. A woman must want very badly to reproduce when she considers all the obstacles in her way. If she has a good life and economic independence, why would she bother?

So what does my story reveal about the choices women 'elders' like me have made? How freely did I choose a childfree life, and do I feel it was worth it? What has been gained, and what lost, by choosing not to give birth and proselytising on behalf of childfreeness? My generation in the developed world was the first to be able to make an informed choice about pregnancy and motherhood – despite the legal and social attacks on this choice. In many countries women and young girls have given birth unwillingly (often as a result of poverty, lack of contraception, rape or coercion) and so have had no ability to 'choose'. I am hugely grateful that I was able to make a choice that has given me a life full of opportunities to teach, write, engage in a range of cultural events, travel, make friends around the world, and relish an adult partnership without the physical and emotional stress and financial cost of children. I know how rare this is for most women. But is my voice contributing to the planet's new 'demographic winter'? Are those of us who remain childless by choice doing our fragile planet a favour (as the renowned environmental campaigner Chris Packham argues), or are we making a decision based on despair and hopelessness? Do we not care about the future of the human race?

And What about the Climate and Global Population Crises?

In 2022, the world population was declared to be eight billion, with a Dominican Republic baby, Dorian, symbolising this milestone, hailed by UN Secretary-General António Guterres as 'an occasion to celebrate'.[3] The satirical magazine *Private Eye* posted two contradictory articles from the *Guardian* newspaper. The first claimed the impact of this rise was 'far-reaching, putting additional pressure on already stretched resources and challenging efforts to reduce poverty and inequality'. The other warned that 'a reproductive crisis' was possible if action was not taken to 'tackle a drop in sperm count' as 'the rate of decline is accelerating'.[4] The Australian government is talking of 'a baby recession'. Ironically, this population milestone marked a decline of new births since 1990, while population 'growth' is due to people living longer. In the UK, we are not replacing ourselves, and more people are dying than being born. In 2024, journalist Rebecca Reid wrote, 'Women are on baby strike, so let's talk terms', suggesting women wanted social and financial compensation, stipends, goodwill gestures, improved working conditions, and of course money.[5] Dream on!

Panics about 'growth' should, according to population experts, focus on the real problems of inequality, greed and waste. And – a factor that always seems introduced into the discussion as an afterthought – women across the world, aware of the burdens and restrictions on their lives of childbirth and family responsibilities, are deciding to limit their family size or not reproduce at all. This is causing alarm in some countries, aware of the danger of being burdened with ageing populations unsupported by a sufficient number of the young and economically active. China's population (ever since the one-child rule) has fallen for the first time in decades, with a demographic crisis of deaths outnumbering births, and a larger number of ageing parents and grandparents than of the young working people required to support them and fuel economic growth. Rebecca Reid might note that offers of financial packages, cash handouts, tax cuts and more have failed to work. In India, a couple who exhausted their savings to raise and educate their son, and organise a lavish wedding, demanded that – six years after the marriage – either their son and his wife produce a grandchild within a year or repay them almost $650,000. The choice of couples (especially women) not to reproduce in a country that has always enjoyed multigenerational households is a clear economic and social threat to a society focused on the family. Women are voting with their wombs . . .

The question is, how can childbearing and child-raising be made appealing as well as lucrative – something that women, not just those in the developed world, know is quite a challenge? Until technology can produce babies outside of women's bodies, and men and women are persuaded and enabled to share equally the heavy financial, emotional and burden of child-rearing, governments won't be able to address the desires and anxieties of the women they wish to be mothers. Anti-abortion commentators feel it's presumptuous, even wicked, for women to claim ownership of our bodies – as if we are only vessels for the next generation. As Adrienne Rich said presciently in 1979, 'Both the Right to Life and the Population Control movements are obsessed with direct control of women's bodies – not with discovering and creating conditions which would make life more liveable for the living.'[6] And Margaret Atwood's chillingly prescient 1985 novel *The Handmaid's Tale* was a reminder that – if women won't cooperate – governments can exert power over us/them to ensure they do nothing but stay home and reproduce. While Atwood's novel and the TV series based on it may seem sensationalist and exaggerated, recent verbal attacks on childless women by the Christian Right and the Trump-Vance Republican Party, as well as the Taliban's virtual imprisonment of Afghan women in the home – excluding them from education, training, and all public spaces and social life – show how easy this can be.

In Britain, the *Sun* newspaper published an article, 'Bonk for Britain', with a Conservative cabinet minister arguing that women should get tax cuts to encourage a baby boom. His xenophobic argument was that the labour shortages we were suffering meant we should have more children. Citing Hungary's tax-cutting policy, he said we need to be 'weaned off our addiction to immigration'.[7] This argument is closely related to the Great Replacement Theory, a set of racist and antisemitic lies and delusions that has cropped up around the world in the past decade. Its central argument – used among others to justify the murders of non-whites in a mosque in Christchurch,

New Zealand (2019) and a supermarket in Buffalo, New York (2022) – claims that white people are being stripped of power through a demographic rise of communities of colour, driven by immigration. In the US there is a conspiracy theory that an elite cabal of Jews and Democrats is 'replacing' white Americans with Black, Hispanic and other people of colour by encouraging immigration and interracial marriage – the end goal being the eventual extinction of the white race. As governments around the world become increasingly paranoid and angry about 'illegal' migration, this jingoistic rhetoric continues to grow and women are expected to reproduce with their own race to keep out 'foreign/alien' blood.

Women continue to face incredulity and hostility as they opt out of motherhood. Official reports have focused on the economic impact of maternity, and pointed out the dangers to future growth and prosperity of especially educated women turning their backs on a maternal role. In the UK alone, women with degrees are twice as likely as non-degree women to remain childless. Women with absorbing careers, steady incomes and aspirational values see clearly the implications of becoming pregnant in a country that – in terms of reliable and safe maternity provision, affordable housing and childcare, reasonable cost of living, and employers' and society's attitudes to babies and young children – falls very far short of making maternity a walk in the park. On 15 January 2023, the *Observer* published an editorial entitled 'How the UK has become a hostile place to have children'.

The statistics are mind-boggling. The average cost of raising a child to the age of eighteen is between £160,000 and £200,000. The UK has the highest childcare costs of any Organisation for Economic Co-operation and Development (OECD) country (costing between one-third and two-thirds of a couple's take-home pay); securing a stable home is financially out of reach for a rising number of people; cuts to tax credits and benefits for low-income families have resulted in the current situation of almost one in three children living in poverty. Labour MP Stella Creasy (banned from breastfeeding in the House of Commons) decried the government's failure to adequately support parents and commented wryly: '[M]others get shamed whatever they do: go out to work and your kids will be feral; work part-time and you're not really committed to your employer; stay at home and you're failing the forces of feminism.'[8] No wonder women are opting out of motherhood or freezing their eggs in the hope that one day they might be able to afford a family. This is a scandal, and one that leaders of all parties seem unable to recognise and confront.

In the light of these economic and social problems, how can I look women in the eye and encourage them to become mothers – when I have evaded the problems so many of them have already faced or are likely to face? Is it impertinent to suggest that other women should think very hard before deciding against motherhood? And yet that is what I wish to do. I've argued earlier in the book that parenthood is what knits you into society and community, and ensures you have to engage in debates about the future – of family life, education, childcare, the planet's survival and more. Even if you are a good citizen, by refusing parenthood you won't be dealing with all these matters in the intense, day-to-day and personal way parents must. Although a cliché of modern political discourse, the reference to 'our children and grandchildren' is a way of reminding us that we are caretakers of the planet for future generations, and our own demise is in many ways insignificant in the face of those coming after us.

I've been in social situations with other childfree people who've cheerfully opted out of social responsibility by saying, 'Oh well, it'll be after my day.' The looming problems of a population that is fast ageing, with numerous minor and major health problems, remind us that all civilised societies must care for their elderly and allow them dignified ageing and death. No wonder the issue of assisted dying is preoccupying us. More than ever, we are living in atomised units with a huge rise in single households. The charity Ageing Without Children warns that many people are growing old without kids for various reasons: they've never had children; their children have died; their children are estranged from them and/or live far away. As they grow older and more frail, these people will eventually need the kind of care that families were expected to provide to their senior members, but which will now need to be administered by professionals, relatives, neighbours or casual helpers. This will require more flexible and imaginative socio-economic solutions to the social-care problem, which politicians continue to fudge while paying syrupy lip service to The Family.

However, for those of us choosing not to create biological families, there are other optimistic scenarios. Maxine Davies refers to Patricia Hill Collins's book *Black Feminist Thought*

(1990), which explores the idea of 'other-mothering' in which Black women engage in 'kin-work' to support mothers' responsibility for caregiving in local neighbourhoods. Community networks, involving childfree women, could and should be strengthened to help support parents to do this most difficult of jobs.[9]

We can embrace the designations Jody Day gives us, 'Crones, Hags and Elder Wise Women of Power', relishing our free and flexible lives without family constraints. And more than ever, children without parents (abandoned, alienated, runaway, migrant and so on) need foster, step- or adoptive parents, while many companion animals need the same. Those without children are in a good position to step in. I've already shown how mothering takes very different forms, and the capacity to mother is welcomed by those in need and is also a source of joy. Indigenous communities survive on horizontal kinship networks that include the childless, and in some British and Irish rural communities women beyond the family are called 'Auntie'. The godparent role is an example of the safety net parents often throw round their children. Earlier I noted sixty-four-year-old adoptive mother Julia Peyton-Jones's selection of thirty-seven godparents, while Germaine Greer has had fourteen godchildren. Lucky kids! Parenting a pet dog or cat, as I've already discussed, is for many a happy alternative to the pram in the hall. No wonder singer Taylor Swift ironically embraced J. D. Vance's name 'childless cat lady' for herself.

As the three Covid lockdowns demonstrated, neighbours and friends were quick to help those without families to survive while enjoying some distanced company. Local and community gatherings – street parties, voluntary organisations, sports groups, food banks, warm spaces in libraries and shops, book clubs, choirs, safe houses – remind us that the traditional family (increasingly rare) is often an unreliable or dangerous place, and certainly not the only forum in which one might feel safe and loved. We are reminded daily of the many children who have to get by with violent, mentally and physically ill, or simply incompetent parents. The challenges of being a mother or father are sentimentalised or smoothed over in so many contexts. And the continuity and legacy a family with children can provide are not the only ways we can leave a mark and secure a place in history. In 'The End of the Line', Tim Kreider argues the childless 'constitute a kind of existential vanguard, forced by our own choices to face the naked question of existence with fewer illusions, or at least fewer consolations, than the rest of humanity, forced to prove to ourselves anew every day that extinction does not negate meaning'.[10] And while that is a rather cold philosophical reflection on childlessness, it echoes my own experience of liberation from the 'family comes first' scenarios I've outlined throughout this book.

So, should we decide the planet is doomed and refuse to bring another generation into the world? How will this help, if what is needed is a galvanisation of populations to demand that nations tackle the huge threats to our climate and rule out nuclear war? Having children gives you a huge investment in and thus concern for the future – so no woman should feel guilty for wanting her own children, biological or not. Life can be long, and as our population grows older, we need to ensure we have close ties – kin and kith who will support, comfort and give us joy (and also fix our computer and online problems for us). What is important is that those with children and those without should offer mutual support and understanding, without the adverse judgements that too often get thrown around. You may envy me my ample time, space and resources, but don't dismiss me as a selfish, narcissistic and sinister witch. I may find all your family photos a bit overwhelming, but I'll help you upstairs with your baby buggy, babysit for you, and also argue on your behalf with politicians that women need much better maternity and childcare provision and pay.

Why are some (usually male) politicians so threatened by the idea of women controlling our own bodies and choosing our own reproductive future, and why do female parents have to bear so much of the brunt of costs and drudgery involved in motherhood? Adrienne Rich asked, 'What would it mean to mother in a society where women were deeply valued and respected, in a culture which was woman-affirming?'[11] Given this is currently a pipe dream, some women are responding to growing institutionalised misogyny and abuse by turning to political lesbianism and/or joining the South Korean-led 4B movement (refusing heterosexual marriage, dating, sex or childbirth). Isn't it therefore rational for my younger sisters to follow my example and refuse to reproduce in this century of climate emergency, population crisis, growth of reproductive technologies, the unstable nature of global politics, the Andrew Tate-led backlash against feminism, and the changing position and aspirations of women across the globe?

I repeat the question asked by US politician Alexandria Ocasio-Cortez: 'Is it okay to still have children?' My answer is that, regardless of the many problems and costs involved in reproduction, wide-scale childlessness may prove a solipsistic threat to social cohesion, our commitment to saving the planet, and our responsibility for the future. In the face of a future threatened by AI and robots, we need to keep our precious human race alive and kicking. But without doubt, what is urgently needed is far more political, financial, emotional and practical support for mothers – and a generous recognition that not every woman is cut out for the job. Following Queen Elizabeth's death in September 2022, Stella Duffy tweeted, '"Mother, grandmother, great grandmother." All good. And if your life doesn't allow any of those things to be said of you on your death – also all good. You count too. All lives count, parent or not.'

Afterword
Literary Childfree Women

I've just told you my own story, and fleshed it out with those personal, cultural and political contexts in which I decided to remain childfree. Yet while thinking and writing about childfreeness, I've reflected on the ways mothers and non-mothers have been represented in art and literature, and how experiencing these has enhanced or hindered my own life decision. All around us are images of mothers and children, and so in this Afterword I draw on a lifetime of reading and literary training to try – very selectively – to trace a pattern in our culture's approaches to the phenomenon of childless/free women.

Mothers are everywhere – from Madonnas in churches and Renaissance paintings, to the Impressionists' family portraits, and iconic images such as Rembrandt's mother, Gustav Klimt's and Mary Cassatt's *Mother and Child*, and Dorothea Lange's *Migrant Mother*. It's hard to paint or photograph an absence, so non-mothers are often represented as workers, servants, childminders or solitary readers. From the Holy Family to the bourgeois family, mother-centred families are the great narrative running through most art forms – from medieval painting to soap opera.

Literature is populated with female characters without children, sometimes resisting the maternal narrative. Childless and childfree female characters recur in fiction, from Jane Austen's Miss Bates, Mrs Gaskell's Cranford community and Dickens's Miss Haversham, to Eudora Welty's southern eccentrics, Agatha Christie's Miss Marple, *A Streetcar Named Desire*'s Blanche DuBois, Martha in *Who's Afraid of Virginia Woolf?*, Miss Jean Brodie and *Hotel du Lac*'s Edith Hope, Sara Paretsky's V. I. Warshawski and Patricia Cornwell's Kay Scarpetta. Often these women are comic or grotesque, figures of pathos or tragedy (rarely heroinic protagonists, except in detective novels). Many novels and films feature single women with dilemmas about marriage, problematic motherhood, abortion, domestic violence and child neglect. What doesn't seem to be in abundance is a variety of childfree female (and occasionally male, unless gay) characters depicted in all their complexity.[1]

Like many readers, I always want to know the marital status and numbers of children of writers in whom I'm interested. Despite decrying the focus of critics and journalists on – mainly women's – private lives, I turn immediately to a book's dedication and acknowledgements to see who has been thanked and what kind of household or relationships formed this book. If writers with large families create a childless protagonist or minor character, I'm interested in how those figures are treated throughout. Some of our greatest women writers had no children: Jane Austen, George Eliot, Charlotte, Anne and Emily Brontë (though ironically Charlotte died in childbirth), Virginia Woolf, Jean Rhys, Eudora Welty, Flannery O'Connor, Simone de Beauvoir, Elizabeth Taylor, Hilary Mantel, Bernardine Evaristo, Jeanette Winterson. Many writers – Mary Wollstonecraft, Doris Lessing, Sylvia Plath, Alice Munro, for example – have had great challenges and conflicts as mothers.

Sigrid Nunez provocatively asks, '[W]ho can name a major novel by a canonical writer, male or female, that takes motherhood for its main subject?'[2] Although I believe she protests too much, I'd like to know who can name a major canonical novel about voluntary childlessness. I want to explore selected, significant works that focus on the childfree to see if I can draw conclusions about how writers over time have grappled with the issue, and to see whether they offer literary role models for women readers like myself.

In the late nineteenth century, the novel that captured the zeitgeist of an era in which childless women began to be a social phenomenon and problem – defined as 'surplus', 'redundant' and 'odd' – was George Gissing's *The Odd Women* (1893). Gissing gave a name to such creatures, and his novel is recognised as the most prominent and influential of the studies of fin-de-siècle 'New Women'. Its focus is on the nature of marriage and the implications of that institution for male-female relationships in a society that had a surfeit of unmarried women with few educational or employment opportunities. The novel features the three Madden sisters – all from a genteel background but impoverished after their improvident father's death – and the ways they face their future. The youngest, Monica, reluctantly marries a man, Edmund Widdowson, who will secure her financial future, but soon finds herself the object of damaging coercive control. The sisters are complemented by two independent women, Rhoda Nunn and Mary Barfoot, who – aware there is a surplus of half a million women in the country – run secretarial training for single women. These, in Nunn's words, are not 'useless, lost, futile lives', but rather 'a great reserve. When one woman vanishes in matrimony, the reserve offers a substitute for the world's work.'[3]

The novel ends with adoptive mother Alice planning to open a school for young children, while Rhoda – still single and pitying her dead sister Monica's orphaned child – plans larger premises for her business and is about to publish a paper. The novel demonstrates the impossibility of marriage for a New Woman, and also the hazards of marriage, notably childbirth. Work and economic independence, as well as freedom from the shackles of marriage, are Gissing's progressive solution for the dignity and survivability of fin-de-siècle women. This is a somewhat sterile and puritanical solution, omitting the need for love, sexual desire and pleasure.

'Odd Women' Fiction

Early in the twentieth century, Gissing's *The Odd Women* was succeeded by other British fictional treatments of 'odd women': novels by writers such as F. M. Mayor, May Sinclair, Dorothy Richardson, Rose Macaulay and George Orwell. Three-quarters of a million British men were killed or badly injured in the Great War, and there was a large gap between male and female populations aged 25–34. The popular press referred to 'The Problem of the Surplus Woman', a gender imbalance since the mid-nineteenth century, though one writer, Dorothy Richardson, celebrated the freedom and autonomy allowed by singlehood and working in an office. However, for many women, doomed to that unenviable state of 'spinsterhood', the economic, emotional and sexual deprivations of impoverished life doing mundane clerical work for the War Office and other government offices were tedious indeed.

In 2022, a novel that had been out of print for a hundred years, Marjorie Grant's *Latchkey Ladies*, was reprinted with a new introduction by critic Sarah LeFanu. The 'latchkey ladies' of the title live in rented 'dismal rooms, being independent and hating it'[4] – very different from the delight in the city by Richardson's Miriam Henderson and Virginia Woolf's Mrs Dalloway. The central figure in *Latchkey Ladies*, Anne Carey, highlights the precariousness and sheer misery of being single, poor and exploited at work – without the promise of a happier future. LeFanu argues that Grant's novel follows other 'redundant women' novels by Dorothy L. Sayers, Rose Macaulay, Dorothy Richardson and Virginia Woolf in asking what kinds of lives are open to women if they don't marry, and how can they find 'love, affection, stability, comfort, economic security and, not least, a meaningful life?' – though she says Grant also asks 'what about sexual desire?'[5] The inevitable result of that desire is a baby conceived out of wedlock, who dies soon after birth. Rather like Gissing's conclusion, Grant makes protagonist Anne wary of further commitment so she will pledge only to a slightly dry cerebral route, learning Greek – with the help of a possible future suitor.

A novel that has spoken to many women, especially since its 1978 reprinting by The Women's Press, is Sylvia Townsend Warner's *Lolly Willowes* (1926). The eccentric and individualistic Lolly is now seen as a feminist icon. Like many novels about single childless women, the absence of a mother and father is striking. Laura Willowes loses her parents, though before his sudden death her father keeps her close. He protects her from her somewhat insensitive older brothers, thinking no man good enough for her, and encourages her engagement with rural pharmacopoeia – even urging her to publish a little book, *Health by the Wayside*. She has no interest in the social graces and feminine wiles required of young marriageable ladies, and instead becomes a passionate reader, preoccupied with botany and brewery. We see early the solitary herbalist she is to become when she roves the countryside for 'herbs and simples'. The irresistible lure of wildness and country lore indicates early on that Laura is never going to settle for bourgeois life. When her father dies, and she is expected to go to live with her brother Henry and family, 'as if she were a piece of family property forgotten in the will . . . ready to be disposed of as they should think best', in a rule-bound and dreary household without a garden, it's clearer than ever that she can never fit into urban life and marriage.

Moving to the country, prompting her brother to predict 'she would start hunting for catnip again, and become the village witch', she discovers a natural affinity with nature, especially the woods where she gathers herbs and then makes brews and distillations. Her unmarried landlady introduces her to the Witches' Sabbath, and she comes to realise 'she was a witch by vocation' – even adopting a black kitten confirming that: 'She, Laura Willowes, in England, in the year 1922, had entered into a compact with the Devil.' Sylvia Townsend Warner plays delightfully with all the tropes of witchcraft and satanism, often associated with childlessness, and throughout she demonstrates how a single woman of independent means is at liberty to move away, leave, walk on her own.

In the final pages of the novel, the fantastical and whimsical nature of Laura's narrative is abandoned for a very long speech to the Devil that could have come straight from *Jane Eyre* or Woolf's *A Room of One's Own.* Laura tells him:

Women have such vivid imaginations, and lead such dull lives. Their pleasure in life is so soon over; they are so dependent upon others, and their dependence so soon becomes a nuisance . . . When I think of witches, I seem to see all over

England, all over Europe, women living and growing old, as common as blackberries, and as unregarded . . . all the time being thrust further down into dullness when the one thing all women hate is to be thought dull.

Commenting on the fact that women have to listen all the time to 'men's things, like politics, or mathematics' and talk of 'the sermon, or war, or cock-fighting' while for them there are 'the potatoes to be cooked for dinner', she complains that 'that sort of thing settles down on one like a fine dust, and by and by the dust is age, settling down'. She claims that while some women may get religion, others – knowing how 'dangerous, how incalculable, how extraordinary they are' – will get witchcraft.[6] The novel ends as Satan leaves her without adverse judgement, and – in a final gesture of freedom from patriarchal and society's constraints – Laura for the first time selects a bed for the night somewhere in the natural world. With Satan's blessing, she becomes a free woman and a witch. No wonder this delightful fantasy has been embraced by modern feminist readers and childfree women.

Virginia Woolf and To the Lighthouse

A novel published one year later than Lolly Willowes is Virginia Woolf's To the Lighthouse (1927), which is set within a family home but reflects Woolf's own obsession with the theme of (excessive and demanding) motherhood.[7] Woolf was advised against having children because of her fragile mental health, and this is a feature or subtext of much of her writing. The charismatic and beautiful central female character, Mrs Ramsay, has eight children – some of whom are hardly named. Partly because of the presence of servants and a relaxed household manner, the children enjoy considerable freedom and hardly get much attention in the text. Certainly Mr Ramsay, a petulant and violent husband, is barely engaged with them; nor it seems are the many artistic and intellectual friends who are invited to the holiday home each summer. None of them – male or female – has children, although all are expected to engage in the family's summer activities.

In one of literature's most startling sudden deaths, Mrs Ramsay dies without explanation about two-thirds of the way through the novel, and we learn that her oldest daughter Prue dies in childbirth shortly afterwards. But childless painter Lily Briscoe survives; she is mesmerised and feels diminished by Mrs Ramsay, who casually asserts that women should marry: '[A]n unmarried woman has missed the best of life. The house seemed full of children sleeping and Mrs Ramsay listening.' Lily thinks that she has her father and her home, 'even, had she dared to say it, her painting. But all this seemed so little, so virginal, against the other.' She wants to express her feelings of being in love, not with Mrs Ramsay herself but with the whole *mise en scène*: '"I'm in love with this all," waving her hand at the hedge, at the house, at the children.'

Through Lily's eyes we see the limitations of Mrs Ramsay as a wife and mother – wanting everyone to marry, pitying William Bankes who after all had 'his work'. But Lily stands between the domestic goddess who reflects on 'the sterility of men', and the single men who have little time for Lily's own 'work'. Charles Tansley's contempt for women who write and paint (they can't, he says) and the disregard other men have for Lily's painting isolate her – and after Mrs Ramsay's death, her widower expects to get Lily's fulsome sympathy. She resists, 'girding at herself bitterly, who am not a woman, but a peevish, ill-tempered, dried-up old maid presumably'. And, despite her grief at Mrs Ramsay's death, Lily feels triumphant that she didn't succumb to her 'limited, old-fashioned ideas . . . this mania of hers for marriage'. In 1927, the year of *Lighthouse*'s publication, Woolf wrote in her diary about her sister Vanessa's children's party, on 20 December. While she says the children's acting 'moved my infinitely sentimental throat', she claims that 'oddly enough I scarcely want children of my own now . . . I don't like the physicalness of having children of one's own . . . I can dramatize myself as a parent, it is true. And perhaps I have killed the feeling instinctively; or perhaps nature does.' But echoing her character Lily, thinking of middle age, she can see how she could become 'a hare-brained egotistic woman, exacting compliments, arrogant, narrow, withered' compared with her sister – against whom she measures herself – who 'takes her way so nonchalantly, modestly, almost anonymously, past the goal, with her children round her'.[8]

In *Talland House* (2020), Maggie Humm offers a contemporary revisionary version of Virginia Woolf's *To the Lighthouse*, with the single, childless painter Lily Briscoe represented in feminist terms as a woman absorbed by her art practice, but also of emotional depths that enrich and complicate her work and life. Speaking to her father (her mother, significantly, is dead), she tells him that marriage may be out of the question because too many eligible men died in the war, and she is content with her friends. She assures him she feels supported by friendships (carefully defined as non-sexual):

[Fellow artist] Emily's ideas had enlarged her world; the Ramsays, she knew, had been a substitute family, Maria and Mrs Beckwith surrogate mothers; and now she and Eliza were two women who saw each other daily, and were together not from any physical attraction but by a shared love of painting, their agreement to continue in a life devoted to art as best they could without complaints, encouraging each other whenever possible, and for as long as they might need to.

When her father asks what she will do when she is his age, she jokes that she'll do the same as him, 'take pleasure in my newspaper, pipe, and tea'.[9] It's interesting that she imagines a masculine older figure, doing male things – there is no role model for an older version of the 'spinster' whom she sees in the mirror every day. But in Humm's version, this is no sad one-dimensional spinster. She has strong sexual desire (alas, hopelessly for a gay man) and she devotes herself to communal work during the war as a nurse. Furthermore, she discovers the secret of Mrs Ramsay's sudden death from arsenic poisoning – revealing the self-destructive nature of this idealised domestic goddess. And in a final triumph of artist over self-sacrificial mother, Lily's painting of Mrs Ramsay is displayed at the Royal Academy. Discovering 'a kind of steady stillness, a future of her own choosing', Lily has come fully into her own, completing her painting with 'the most radiant precious sky Lily could possibly paint, an immense golden glow shimmering over sea and land'.[9]

'A small square of ivory': Barbara Pym and Elizabeth Taylor

A writer who took a wry look at women on the edge of society and – as Anne Tyler put it – 'the heartbreaking silliness of everyday life' – was Barbara Pym. A mid-twentieth-century woman writer of modest reputation who was sidelined as somewhat old-fashioned in the 1960s and whose work went out of print, she was 'rediscovered' by two prestigious male writers, Philip Larkin and Lord David Cecil, who chose her as one of the most underrated novelists of the century. Her best novel, *Excellent Women* (1952), was reprinted in 2009 by Virago Press, with an introduction by Alexander McCall Smith. In his framing of the novel, McCall Smith echoes those descriptions and critiques of Jane Austen that have equated women's lives and narratives with the minor – the small matters of life. 'Pym painted her pictures on a small square of ivory . . . the details of smallish lives led in places that could only be in England'; 'her highly individual, small-scale novels, each of them a little gem'; 'small-scale delights . . . brilliant miniaturisation'. The word 'little' recurs, though he does conclude by arguing that though the novel is 'on one level about very little, [it] is a great novel about a great deal'.[10]

That 'littleness' is something Pym herself flags in the novel with a wryly ironic dig at current fiction, echoing George Eliot's *Middlemarch*'s famous last lines about the world depending on 'unhistoric acts' and those 'who lived faithfully a hidden life, and rest in unvisited tombs'.[11] In a dispute between teachers over wearing hats in chapel, Pym's first-person narrator, Mildred Lathbury, wonders about the amount of energy expended in such a fight, then comments, 'I told myself that, after all, life was like that for most of us – the small unpleasantnesses rather than the great tragedies; the little useless longings rather than the great renunciations and dramatic love affairs of history or fiction.' And, in a comic scene featuring Mildred and the two men who compete to seek her attention, she reflects bitterly of herself, 'the fussy spinster in me, the Martha', that 'if I ever wrote a novel it would be of the "stream of consciousness" type and deal with an hour in the life of a woman at the sink'.[12]

McCall Smith's most perceptive comment about the writer is his description of a 'Barbara Pym moment' which occurs 'when one realises that for those whom one is observing, one will never be an object of love'.[13] It's a study of childless women, some single, some married, living in genteel distressed circumstances in post-World War II London, sharing a bathroom. Mildred offers a view of herself that – parodying Jane Austen – echoes social attitudes to singletons at the time. With a careful use of qualifiers, she provides a sardonic critique of a woman's place: 'I suppose an unmarried woman just over thirty, who lives alone and has no apparent ties, must expect to find herself involved or interested in other people's business, and if she is also a clergyman's daughter then one might really say that there is no hope for her.' This is the first page of the novel, and on the third she describes herself, by contrast with her glamorous married fellow tenant, Mrs Helena Napier, as 'mousy and rather plain . . . with my shapeless overall and old fawn skirt', but – in a reference to Jane Eyre, 'who must have given hope to so many plain women who tell their stories in the first person' – she refuses to accept any comparison.

Ironically, readers will indeed make connections, with both women intelligent homeless orphans of no great beauty who have to carve out their own lives and maintain their Christian faith. Mildred's work for the Society for the Care of Aged Gentlewomen echoes Jane's job as a governess, though in the former case there is no Mr Rochester, just two rather eccentric men drawn to her but without romantic intentions (one given the name Rockingham, which comically echoes Rochester's). From the beginning, we recognise that this narrator is not naive and is well aware of others' perceptions and the way a woman such as herself is generally perceived. Of her weekly laundry, she comments, 'Just the kind of underclothes a person like me might wear, I thought dejectedly, so there is no need to describe them.'

Given the fact that the church supports families, Pym's Mildred participates in church services dominated by 'elderly ladies and dim spinsters' – the 'Miss Enders, Miss Statham and . . . Mrs Morris' at the jumble-sale tea urn. Words like 'sensible' and 'practical' are attached to Mildred, and men define women like her as 'excellent', meaning sexless, dull, unmarriageable – compared with the showy, narcissistic and fairly unpleasant women who offer sex appeal to men (Mrs Napier, Mrs Gray). But the novel throbs with Mildred's own suppressed erotic longings and sexual desire, and her repeated disappointments as she is expected to make tea and wash dishes for others. When Rocky (Rockingham) tells her how she loves 'contriving things . . . Births, deaths, marriages and all the rest of it', she acknowledges to herself the truth: 'perhaps I really enjoyed other people's lives more than my own'. The novel concludes with Mildred's competence and 'sensible' nature being rewarded, if not by declarations of love then at least by calls on her time, so that it seems she may have what Helena called '"a full life" after all'.[14]

In a novel written in the last period of her life, *Quartet in Autumn* (1977, reprinted in 2015), Pym creates a group of single people – two men and two women, one widowed – who work together in an office during the 1970s doing undefined and clearly rather meaningless jobs, and who are all on the cusp of retirement. The women retire (the statutory age being then lower than men's) and their fortunes are followed as they face the blank spaces of lives without partners or children. There are excruciating descriptions of those key family occasions that have no meaning for the four – Mother's Day and Christmas – and the fear of existing and dying alone is ever present. Pym's cynicism about family life emerges in her description of the Christmases all four choose. Edwin reflects on the fact that people are apt to say, 'Christmas is a time for the children', and he reluctantly goes to his son's (though he would have preferred to stay at home, go to church services and have a drink with Father G). Norman feels uncomfortable about going to his brother's, who has a new partner. Both women suffer from the pity, or imagined pity, of others: Marcia's neighbour invites her to Christmas dinner which Marcia fails to eat, and Letty is reluctantly forced to eat with her landlady.

Letty is an impoverished and timidly puritanical woman who has a quiet fantasy life enhanced by regular lunches out of the office and novel reading. Pym makes an ironic comment on her own profession and indeed her own characters. As she nears retirement, Letty 'had come to realize that the position of an unmarried, unattached, ageing woman is of no interest whatsoever to the writer of modern fiction'. Her retirement plans to share a country home with an old female friend are upended when the friend becomes engaged, so she throws herself into reading sociology books from the library (a big mistake, she decides), takes a little holiday, resolves against drinking sherry before the evening or reading a novel in the morning, and responds positively to Edwin and Norman's invitation to lunch – bought with luncheon vouchers from the office. Having resigned herself to an old age in the country living near her affianced friend Marjorie, she reneges on this plan after Marjorie's fiancé dumps her, and so Letty resolves to remain in London – a bold decision which seems life-affirming. She then organises a country visit with Edwin and Norman, making her realise 'life still held infinite possibilities for change'.

There is one crucial moment in the novel when Letty glimpses a communal, multicultural and vibrant life possibility after knocking on the door of her landlord's flat to ask Mr Olatunde, the Nigerian priest of a religious sect, to make a little less noise. In an episode that makes a modern race-conscious reader squirm, she is invited into his flat by him, asked if she is a Christian lady, and offered supper by his wife. Olatunde's vibrant erotic energy, to which Letty clearly responds, points up her own anaemic personality and life. She finds it impossible to explain to 'this vital, ebullient black man her own blend of Christianity – a grey, formal, respectable thing of measured observances and mild general undemanding kindness to all'.[15] Like *Excellent Women*, this novel focuses on modest, ordinary people who hover on the margins of what might be regarded as normal life, and all feel dissociated from and tangential to orthodox families. Their childlessness is a key feature in the novel, but by the end Pym offers them all (single and childless men and women alike) a kind of camaraderie of the dispossessed.

A writer often coupled in popular imagination with Pym, sharing her delicious irony and sense of the absurd, is the (belatedly) critically acclaimed Elizabeth Taylor. Two of her novels focus on unorthodox childfree women. *Angel* (1957) is a sardonic, witty study of Angel Deverell, a working-class girl who – to the astonishment of her mother and aunt – lives inside her own imagination (lying a lot) and aspires to be a great sensational romantic novelist in the style of other successful, independent childless Edwardian women writers such as Marie Corelli and Rhoda Broughton. She begins to write, serendipitously finds a tolerant and kind publisher, and achieves critical ignominy but popular success as – in Hilary Mantel's words – 'high priestess of schlock'.[16] Her aunt Lottie works as a lady's maid at the grand Paradise House which she yearns to inhabit, and – as she becomes commercially successful – finally buys and then neglects badly. Showing no interest in real romance or sex, let alone a family life, the socially awkward, self-absorbed Angel constructs a romantic ideal for the man she marries, an avaricious and hypocritical painter, Esmé, who expects her to pay his bills and give him the life of leisure he craves. Angel is unkempt and unworldly, relying on her sister-in-law Nora – whose poetic career has to be abandoned – to run her household and take care of the feckless and unfaithful Esmé.

The couple have no children, and neither does Angel's publisher Theo. After Esmé dies, Theo reflects on how little of him remains, except for the half-finished memorial Angel has constructed, a small collection of paintings in an unused studio, and Angel's 'crazed and persistent' love. But this is perhaps all one can expect as – 'utterly depressed' – Theo ruminates on Esmé and his dead wife Hermione: 'As we grow older, we are already dying; our hold on life lessens; there are fewer to mourn us or keep us in mind.'[17] This is a sober tale about the fading of childless lives, and the limited legacy they leave behind. Angel's early writing success fades as she goes out of fashion; her husband's paintings have no market; the literary world is no kind of emotional or indeed financial support unless you keep churning out stuff. The large number of uncontrolled cats Angel keeps in her shabby, chaotic, ironically named Paradise House – with only Silky Boy curled up against her as she dies – is a metaphor for the solipsistic life of a writer without significant legacy. Hilary Mantel, herself a childless writer, reads from this novel that Taylor is telling us 'Writers are monsters'. Is Mantel suggesting Angel's monstrosity derives from her writerly self-absorption, of which childlessness is also a symptom? She doesn't explain.

In one of her last novels, *Mrs Palfrey at the Claremont* (1971), Taylor takes an even bleaker view of women's ageing without children. In a respectable but dreary Kensington hotel, some women – Mrs Palfrey included – have children, but none of them receives visits from them or grandchildren, relying on occasional visits from relatives (or in the case of Miss Benson, a 'well known woman in her time', none at all). Mrs Palfrey, one of the most glamorous, has a daughter Elizabeth with whom she exchanges letters that 'were either a farce or a formality', and she boasts that her grandson Desmond will come for dinner – a source of some excitement in the hotel. But he never does, so Mrs Palfrey passes off as her grandson a young man, Ludo, who rescues her after a street fall. Their slowly burgeoning friendship offers her pleasure, and status within the Claremont, and she considers changing her will to leave him the inheritance her negligent grandson was to receive. She tells Ludo that when she was a young woman she longed to be free 'of nursery chores and social obligations, one's duty', and her sad conclusion is that the only way of being free is 'to be not needed' – something which is challenged when Ludo claims that he needs her. In a poignant reflection by one of the hotel's absent-minded and forgetful guests, 'It was hard work being old. It was like being a baby, in reverse. Every day for an infant means some new little thing learned; every day for the old means some little thing lost. Names slip away, dates mean nothing, sequences become muddled, and faces blurred.'[18] To age, without the obligations of and responsibilities for a younger generation, is sad indeed.

Twentieth-Century Middlebrow Treatments of the Childfree: Margaret Forster, Penelope Lively, Margaret Drabble

But things change. The generational differences Taylor alludes to are developed in later writers' work. As the century moved on, women became more assertive as the women's movement gathered strength, and family divisions erupted. Margaret Forster, obsessively engaged with family and domestic life herself, was acclaimed for her unsentimental explorations of family conflicts in late twentieth-century family life. In *Private Papers* (1987), her protagonist Penelope Butler writes accounts of her life which are discovered and read by her daughter Rosemary. An abandoned baby herself, who grows up in a home, Penelope marries a doctor and has three daughters with her husband, who goes missing, presumed dead, in World War II. She adopts another baby, who later dies, and in midlife goes to work for an adoption society. For her adult life, family and family values are what keep her going, and she devotes herself to keeping her daughters together, welcoming them home after their various disastrous life decisions and actions, and firmly believing that the institution of family should be valued above all else – despite much evidence from her daughters to the contrary.

Oldest daughter Rosemary, exasperated at and challenging her mother in every way, debunks the idea that family love is 'unconditional. Nobody bargained in a family, nobody said they would love you if you stopped truanting or shop-lifting or whatever, they just loved you. Well, Mother may have believed that load of crap. None of the rest of us did.' The trajectory of the daughters' lives (and one death) tells a story of changing mores, attitudes to marriage and children, and the sentimentality that often surrounds mother-daughter relationships.

Rosemary angrily repudiates Penelope's dignified support and forgiveness of her children – especially when all the daughters returned home or relied on Penelope to shelter, coddle and help them in dire times. Rosemary's final defiant words, wondering how to deal with all the private papers she's read, are to say she had 'walked all over [Penelope's] memories, opinions and judgements' and thus was a 'trespasser without mercy'.[19] How true that must feel for many a daughter wanting to distance herself from, and in some ways annihilate, her own mother. It's a remarkably bitter and uncompromising conclusion.

In recent decades, writers have chosen female protagonists who unashamedly opt for a single, childless route. Penelope Lively's novel *Spiderweb* (1998), features Stella, a retired single, childless academic anthropologist who decides to retire to a Somerset village. At sixty-five, she is conscious of being free to determine her own destiny – after a peripatetic and emotionally complicated working life. She points out that in other societies, 'the likes of her would be variously seen as valuable repositories of knowledge, as objects of pity and respect, or as economic encumbrances ripe for disposal'. She and her lesbian friend Judith, who have worked as professional observers in different countries and been objects of interest and suspicion, agree that unmarried and childless women would have been burned as witches in other times and places, or consulted as oracles. As anthropologists, they agree not having children might make them 'freaks'. Stella says, 'The norm is to stake out your claim in the kinship network, establish your credentials by way of offspring. Get yourself into the gene pool,' while Judith refutes that: 'It's simply a system to ensure a controllable labour supply.'[20] The novel demonstrates both the threat a woman like Stella can pose to others (the local children take against her and shoot her dog) and also the attractiveness of her independence to those who seek support and companionship in old age. I like the fact that Lively concludes the novel by giving Stella new freedom guiltlessly to reject all ties.

Margaret Drabble, whose earlier work did so much to bring attention to the problems and conflicts of mothers, offers a darkly comic perspective on the childlessness issue. In *The Dark Flood Rises* (2016), the protagonist's enigmatic daughter Poppet, who gets on badly with her mother, is described by her father in the classic way a certain kind of singleton often is: 'Earnest, in his view humourless, and probably cleverer than her brother, she is obsessed by the imminent death of the planet. She works for an environmental agency, processing statistics. She tells him she's a neo-Malthusian, whatever that may be. She has no children.' Mind you, her much older mother Fran – who has an uncomfortable distanced relationship with both Poppet and her son Christopher – reflects on herself: 'Old grannies. Old crones. She is one of them now, she has joined their haggard company, those Grimm words are her indicators.'[21] How stark this generational difference between women seems: the optimism and social engagement of the younger compared with the mordant self-loathing of the older.

Contemporary Writers

Women with children inevitably compare their lives with those of childless women. Of all the women writers focusing on children, marriage and family life, and comparing her own life with that of the childfree, Rachel Cusk has perhaps divided opinion more than most. Choosing to write honestly and angrily about being a mother, she has drawn warm praise and cold criticism in equal measure. She is clear about her writerly resentments:

I have a romantic conception of the writer's life and the sort of writer's life that I admire is probably a childless life, possibly a marriageless life, certainly a travelling life – I'm in awe of how much DH Lawrence managed to get around. But that's never been something I'm capable of doing. All I've ever done is work really hard, try and try and try to put down roots, marry and have children and lead this completely stable life.[22]

In *A Life's Work* (2001), there is a spectre lurking: the childless woman, she of the considerable wealth and privilege of an Edith Wharton: 'She married, a marriage of class and convenience, but lived separately, estranged, and finally on a different continent from her husband . . . [she had] a large collection of lapdogs . . . and she found philanthropy: living in France during the First World War, she set up refuges and schools for orphaned children'. In the Introduction, Cusk has a 'gloomy suspicion' that such a book is of real interest only to mothers: 'the experience of motherhood loses nearly everything in its translation to the outside world'.

She suggests that people might not have children if they knew what it was like, and claims: 'People without children certainly don't seem very interested in anything that people with have to say about it: they approach parenthood blithely, as if they were the first, with all the innocence of Adam and Eve before the fall.' And with barely suppressed anger she refers to childless people (friends?), who come round just before going to a party, say they've been in bed for three days with a cold, and 'conspicuously do not say "why don't I take the baby so that you can have some time off?"' Later, writing about moving around a city with a baby like 'a very large rucksack' that she can leave nowhere because she is 'the baby's home', she begins 'to look at those who walk around light and free and unencumbered as if they were members of a different species'. And this sense of being encumbered and a different species leads her to 'see something inhuman in civilisation, something vain and deadly . . . its greed, its lack of charity'.[23] Cusk articulates with brutal honesty a deep resentment held by burdened mothers towards non-mothers they perceive to be completely free.

In *Things I Don't Want to Know* (2013), Deborah Levy describes a visit to Majorca on the trail of George Sand, where she is intrigued by the independent-minded woman Maria who runs a largely solo-traveller hotel, which Levy sees a as 'a refuge from The Family'. Biting into a breakfast apricot Maria has brought her, she reflects on Maria's life 'that did not include the rituals of marriage and motherhood' and – echoing Rachel Cusk – Levy thinks of the women who joined her to wait for their children in the school playground: 'Now that we were mothers we were all shadows of our former selves, chased by the women we used to be before we had children.' Quoting Julia Kristeva's *Motherhood Today*, Levy claims that 'motherhood is imbued with what has survived of *religious feeling*'. She continues: 'Mother was The Woman the whole world had imagined to death. It proved very hard to re-negotiate the world's nostalgic phantasy about our purpose in life.' For Levy, 'Mother' was a delusion 'imagined and politicised by the societal system'.[24] Isn't it fascinating and terrifying that both childless women and mothers are the focus of endless fantasies that bear little relationship to material reality?

American writer Ann Patchett is renowned for her fiction and essays about family life, marriage, female friendship and dogs. *The Dutch*

House (2019) is a work about biological, surrogate and substitute motherhood and family relations. It's narrated by Danny Conroy, whose closest lifelong relationship is with his older sister, Maeve, who cares for and guards him like a mother. After their real mother leaves the family to go to help people in India, and then never returns, the siblings' closeness is crucial, no more so than when their father remarries. After his death, their hostile stepmother throws them out of the house. For the rest of their adult lives Maeve is the self-sacrificial one who ignores the dangers of her own diabetes, enables Danny's expensive medical education, then supports his move into property development. Danny marries, but his wife occupies a lukewarm place in his heart compared with his sister, and significantly Maeve never marries or has children.

Not surprisingly, she is treated with suspicion and jealousy by her sister-in-law, Celeste, who exploits her and expects Danny to disregard her autonomy. 'What was never said but was perfectly clear was that Maeve had no husband, no children, and so her time was less valuable.' And significantly, neither of the cruel stepmother's children, Norma and Bright, has children. 'Norma said that childhood wasn't something she could imagine inflicting on another person, especially not a person she loved.' But, in a conciliatory gesture following Maeve's sudden death – perhaps aware of the absence of family she now faces as she moves back to California – Norma suggests to Danny that she could be his sister. While the pull of biological relationships is seen to damage or hold back female autonomy, Patchett acknowledges alternative ways of constructing family bonds.[25]

Ann Patchett has no children, and her 2021 essay collection *These Precious Days* included a piece titled 'There Are No Children

Here'. While telling stories about her joy at watching a birth, and a spontaneous desire to adopt a homeless child (which came to nothing), she describes a literary life of book tour appearances and interviews in which she is often asked why she has no children. A male writer tells her that you can't be a real writer unless you have children – and when she asks why not, he replies, 'Because until you have children, you don't know what it means to love.' Wryly, she observes that the comments echo those of people who ask why you don't drink alcohol – as if it is a judgement on those who do. 'People want you to want what they want,' she says. She is given warnings by strangers. A radio host asks if she worries about being alone at the end of her life. Another woman tells her she should have a child even if she doesn't want one, because 'later on you'll wish you had one, and then it will be too late'. A probation officer who collects her on a book tour tells her it took two years to get a doctor to agree to perform a tubal ligation because every doctor she consulted told her she'd change her mind.[26] Ann Patchett herself has always been clear that she wanted to be a writer, and lacked the energy to do that, everything else, and also have children.

Millennial Perspectives

In the twenty-first century, millennial writers are increasingly foregrounding issues around women's choice in relation to marriage and childbirth. In Emma Gannon's novel *Olive* (2020), a group of four best friends who've been close since childhood move through adulthood together making different life choices. The first-person narrator, Olive, is a journalist, then editor of *.dot* magazine. Certain she doesn't want to have children, she's commissioned to write an article about why women make that choice. It hadn't occurred to her that her closest friends would make different decisions. Her first realisation of this is when she and her friend Bea take pregnancy tests at the same time (both negative), and Olive is startled to realise Bea is sad that hers isn't positive. Bea later has two children, Cecily is joyfully pregnant and holds a pre-birth baby shower, while Isla has a series of unsuccessful IVF treatments. The tensions around and between all four of them become increasingly apparent as Olive's desolation at her relationship break-up is softened by time and a new romance. Olive admits to an 'unnerving' feeling when in the company of two or more women who are mothers: 'They have this unifying, unbreakable bond that I can't compete with. It's as if they have an invisible thread that ties them so closely together.' Her only comparable experience is cat-sitting and putting out food a few times a day.

The novel's appeal to modern women lies, I suspect, in the seriousness with which Olive treats her female friendships and the importance she places on keeping them flourishing despite their different life choices regarding children. The fact they are all white middle-class professionals means there are no articulated class or race conflicts, and the online responses to this book suggest Gannon has reached young confused women with her story of representative figures. The novel's resolution, with Olive finding a new older lover who's already a father, is upbeat in affirming the creation of alternative families: 'We make our own family – kids, friends, pets, neighbours, strangers, passions, memories – and we can shape other people's lives in so many ways.'[27] The choice of women friends (rather than whether or not to be a mother) is confirmed as the most important choice she makes.

A book that has been hailed as one of the most important contributions to the fraught debates around childbearing is Sheila Heti's

Motherhood (2018). Described as a novel, it reads more like a complex philosophical and mystical memoir. A woman of thirty-seven, living with a partner who already has a child, approaches what many see as the reproduction cut-off point of forty – recounting her thoughts, reflections and child-focused dreams about being a mother. Bizarrely, following the I Ching, she resorts to throwing three coins. There is anguished internal debate about whether she wants kids ('the greatest secret I keep from myself'), and the fear of what this may do to her relationship, when her partner makes it clear it is *her* choice. She admits to feeling like a draft dodger from an army in which her friends are serving. But she is clear that – given a choice between a child and a soulmate – she would choose the latter.

Heti writes: 'There is a kind of sadness in not wanting the things that give so many other people their life's meaning . . . there is a bit of a let-down feeling when the great things that happen in the lives of others – you don't actually want those things for yourself'. She suggests people without children could be seen not to move forward, change and grow. As a Jewish woman, she knows she is expected to repopulate for the losses of the Holocaust. But provocatively she says she doesn't really care if the human race dies out, and she suggests no more people for a hundred years – thus no more aggressors and victims. As a writer, she sees her legacy as making art rather than babies, but realises there are so many feelings in play and – as so often in women's writing on the subject – not least her feelings about her own mother.

In a passage that anticipates the 2022 Supreme Court decision reversing *Roe v. Wade*, Heti describes a doctor who was reluctant for her to have an abortion at twenty-one, and reflects on people who wish to forbid abortions, concluding they want women 'to be doing the work of child-rearing more than they want her to be doing anything else. There is something threatening about a woman who is not occupied with children. What is she going to do instead? What sort of trouble will she make?' Her partner Miles emphasises how hard it is to have children, and argues you cannot be a great artist as well as a parent – cultures having held places for those who don't want children, such as nuns and priests, scholars and artists. She describes an American woman saying that a woman can't just say she doesn't want a child. 'You have to have some big plan or idea of what you're going to do instead. And it better be something great.'

But she has a certain romanticism about maternity. She tells the mother of a two-year-old that whatever happens, she has 'this person, this thing' – only to be told that the mother has nothing any more, including her work, and her daughter is her own person, not someone who belongs to her. In a life without a child, 'no one knows anything about your life's meaning . . . Your life's value is invisible,' and she suggests rather surprisingly that maybe motherhood 'means honoring one's mother'.[28]

Another Jewish writer who wished to 'understand why [being single and childfree] works for me' is Israeli author and playwright Sarah Blau. Her crime novel, *The Others* (2022), grapples with the question of what makes women decide not to have children, and whether they should be punished for making this choice. Like Sheila Heti, she has to address the problem of a Jewish woman not wishing to renew her race, and like Heti her response is both defensive and religiously challenging. Blau confronts the modern childfree ethos with the ancient Jewish myth associated with biblical figures who chose a life without children, and narrates the story through the eyes of Sheila, who initially appears to be the murderer of one of her oldest friends, Dina. The novel's title refers to a group of four female students, 'The Others', Dina, Ronit, Naama and Sheila, who – going against their culture's norms and pressures – resolve as a group never to marry or have children, and seal the deal with snake's tongue lipstick that presages blood.

It emerges later that two of the women went against the communal agreement and were either pregnant or undertaking IVF. In a country and city (Tel Aviv) which found wilful childlessness threatening, a lecture on 'Childfree by Choice: Women without Children' is interrupted by a naked doll thrown into the room with the words 'Mummy dearest' in red ink on its forehead. Three of the four women are murdered by a serial killer, with each victim found tied to a chair, a baby doll glued to their hands and the word 'mother' carved on their foreheads. The only survivor, Sheila, the first-person narrator, is the prime suspect for much of the novel, called 'the witch' on the street and in college.

The Others had given provocative quotations in interviews, with Ronit calling childbirth 'a national obsession, a cult that borders on terrorism', claiming she had 'no intention of becoming a reproductive assembly line, I have far more interesting things to do'. She even dressed as the child-devouring Lilith. 'I am the childless mother who eats her young.'

A group discuss the murder of one of The Others, Dina, while one man claims she was guilty of thinking only about herself and 'the hell with your country! . . . Look who's procreating round here, only the Arabs and the Haredim.' Sheila gradually comes to realise the choice of four young students was a 'juvenile gesture' ensuring their difference from everyone else, and that what was right for their youth isn't necessarily right for adult life. She recalls Dina considering the question of leaving something behind, 'a part of you will live on, that you'll be remembered'– and she reflects on the reason childless Hercule Poirot and Miss Marple never had kids and became detectives, 'not to leave your own traces, but to track the trace left by someone else'. When Sheila finally confronts the murderer, she realises that friends are 'not family, and friends of your mother's are certainly not family – only your family is family, only your family is forever, and if for some reason you choose not to have one, there's a good chance you'll end up alone'. This bleak conclusion to a dystopian novel is tempered by the establishment of a new relationship between narrator and murderer, and the rather sentimental claim that there are 'all kinds of relationships. All kinds of love.'[29] I can only imagine how this novel will be received and interpreted since the tragic events in Israel and Gaza following 7 October 2023.

Perhaps the best known 'millennial' writer is Sally Rooney, whose first three novels were praised for being 'the voice of a generation' exploring the preoccupations of white middle-class women trying to forge new ways of living and loving through a world of meaninglessness, climate crisis and social chaos. In *Beautiful World, Where Are You* (2021), best friends Alice and Eileen have complicated email and text exchanges with each other and on-off sexual relationships with complex men. Alice has become a rich and famous thirty-year-old singleton novelist and this has led to a minor breakdown in New York. With Eileen, a literary reviewer, there is shared correspondence about issues ranging from climate change and Christianity to love and sexuality, as well as the purpose (or not) of writing at all.

Both are preoccupied with the challenge of marriage and children, with Alice recognising that women of their age – who in earlier periods would have married and started families – now live alone or with flatmates they never see, 'a sad sterile foreclosure on the possibility of life'. Her conclusion is that having torn down old ways of living, there is 'almost nothing left that makes life worthwhile . . . the easiest way to live is to do nothing, say nothing, and love no one'. By the end of the novel (spoiler alert!), Rooney offers us a different picture of love, with Alice and Felix cohabiting, and Eileen settling down joyfully with Simon, long-term friend and practising Catholic, about to have a baby. Referring both to the fear of giving birth in a global pandemic and the long-term threat of climate change, Eileen says she considered an abortion but decided it would be 'a sort of sick, insane thing to do, a way of mutilating my real life as a gesture of submission to an imagined future'. Having a baby allows her to 'prove that the most ordinary thing about human beings is not violence or greed but love and care', and she concludes by sending love to Alice and proclaiming that she's very happy.[30] This 'happy ending' proved both frustrating and surprising to critics and readers, anticipating from this Marxist writer a more radical and open-ended dénouement – more fitting for that millennial generation for whom she seemed to have spoken. Whether deliberately ironic, or designed to upset critical expectation, Rooney's ending seems to echo Heti's sentiment that having children is a gesture of faith, respect for earlier generations and a refusal of cynicism. Thus Rooney's conclusion is a startling, perhaps perverse gesture of hope and faith in a world that seems locked into perpetual gloom.

A Utopian Vision

A far more optimistic, indeed utopian, vision of childlessness and families is offered by Stella Duffy. More baby boomer than millennial, as a queer woman who has had cancer twice and as a result is infertile, she is interested in the comparison between families of blood and families of choice, including queer families. Until recently, she hadn't realised her seventeen books are all about family creation, despite the fact her own biography bears this out. As one of seven children, of whom five are female, she has fifteen nieces and nephews, thirty-one great-nieces and -nephews. She is deeply involved with them all, though she admits to feeling pain when a friend had her second grandchild. She praises Jody Day's coining of the term 'a pro-natalist society', her recognition of the taboo on queer women having children, and Day's Gateway Women organisation for its constructive and practical approach to childlessness.

In her 2021 novel *Lullaby Beach* (2021), Duffy celebrates what she calls 'diagonal' relationships outside mother-daughter, namely between aunts and nieces, and sisters. The novel begins with the suicide of Aunt Kitty, whose nieces vied for her love and attention, and who ended her life childless. Her great-niece's closeness to her childless aunt Sara creates considerable tension among them all (especially in relation to the suicide). This is very much a 'Me Too' novel describing the ways men of a certain generation exerted coercive control over women of considerable vulnerability and shame. Male violence is eventually challenged and faced down by the strong community of women whose own destructive rage gets free rein. Duffy's narrative doesn't skate over the jealousies, resentments and anger between the women, who all deceive and keep secrets from one another. But female family solidarity in the end counters patriarchal power and exploitation, affording a special place for the childless and childfree.

Is Childfreeness a Concern of Only White Writers?

By now, you must be wondering why all the writers discussed are white (and indeed middle- or lower-middle-class). Despite my best endeavours, I can find almost no novels by working-class, Black, Asian or mixed-race women that celebrate childfree-ness. For obvious reasons, deciding against motherhood is surely a transgression too far for all those women living within strict religious regimes and families, and/or for whom children are one of the only joys in life and signifiers of status. As I discussed in Chapter 7, for Black women who endured enforced parenthood through rape in slavery, or under South Africa's apartheid regime, and have been accused of over-breeding in ways that threaten white hegemony, refusing to reproduce (or choosing to have sex with white men) is to be an outcast, a danger to the future of the race. There is a notable exception.

Toni Morrison's *Sula* (1973) demonstrates all too clearly the toll exacted on a woman who behaves sexually like a man: stealing other women's husbands, then loving and leaving, refusing to marry and to bear children. Sula comes from a beleaguered and dysfunctional community and family in which her grandmother kills her son, Plum; and Sula's mother – who is overheard saying she loves but doesn't like Sula – dies after accidentally setting herself on fire (watched by Sula). As a child, Sula swings a clumsy child round and accidentally drops him to his death in deep water. This happens while she is playing with her only close friend, Nel, who stays in their poor neighbourhood to marry and have children. Sula escapes for a decade, goes to college, has many affairs including with white men, and returns to reap havoc on her neighbours. She steals husbands and stays aloof from the community, which becomes more closely knit in opposition to this estranged woman, led by the men who condemn her sleeping with white men. Sula's grandmother Eva tells her she needs to marry and have some babies ('It'll settle you'). Sula's response is 'I don't want to make somebody else. I want to make myself' – a reply that Eva calls 'selfish'.

As accidents or strange incidents occur in the community, she – with a strong birthmark on her face – is called (predictably) a witch and a devil. Her old friend Nel, whose husband she stole, scolds her, saying she can't have or do it all, or act like a man. Nel and Sula's honest, painful conversation at Sula's deathbed gives voice to the conflicting needs and desires of women, as well as the jealousy of a wife and mother for her friend's ability to escape the trappings of orthodox femininity. Sula defends herself: 'You say I'm a woman and coloured. Ain't that the same as being a man?' Nel replies that she doesn't think so, 'and you wouldn't either if you had children'. Sula's response is that every man she ever knew left his children, and she justifies her behaviour on the grounds that every coloured woman is 'dying like a stump. Me, I'm going down like one of those redwoods. I sure did live in this world.' Called 'lonely', Sula retorts that her lonely 'is *mine*'. Nel's jealous anger explodes when she says to Sula, 'You own the world and the rest of us is renting. You ride the pony and we shovel the shit.' After the 'burial of a witch', there is an assumption that Sula's death will heal all wounds. In fact, the community is broken up, and the novel ends with Nel realising too late it is not her husband she misses, but her unique friend Sula.[31]

The writers I've discussed are or were young and middle-aged. It's rare to find novels or memoirs about childfreeness by older women. Diana Athill is an exception, and her prizewinning *Somewhere Towards the End* (2008) bravely discusses her ambivalence towards having a child. Following an earlier abortion, at the age of forty-three and after carelessness about contraception and unconscious desire, she conceived and felt happy, 'with a happiness so astonishingly complete that I still remember it with gratitude'. After initial joy, Athill had a miscarriage that almost killed her, and she admits with great honesty that the grief of losing the child was swept away by her delight at still being alive. She decides that the experience was 'chemical: the body responding to the approach of menopause by pumping out more of something or other which I don't usually have much of, and after the shock ceasing to pump so that my normal condition was re-established'. This is not a tragic story of waking up too late to the realisation she had lost the ability to bear a child. She notes that she would have been a perfectly adequate mother, but in old age is more interested in and delighted by babies and little children because she doesn't have the hassle of looking after them. She puts this down to selfishness, which wouldn't allow her to give her whole self to a child.[32] For me, she recalls Kate Chopin's Edna Pontellier (*The Awakening*) telling her child-centred friend Adèle that she would give up the unessential, but she would never sacrifice herself for her children.[33] Athill's regret, or shame, is not about her own non-children, but about her cousin Barbara, who was left as a single parent of three. Barbara didn't ask for her help because she was aware of Athill's 'coldness towards her brood'. This causes Athill to feel shame and reminds us that others all too often see the childless as detached, sterile, cold. And in some circumstances they are absolutely right.

• • •

Women who become mothers, whatever their circumstances, are central to a society organised around the family. Childless or childfree women, like those around them, are always aware of their status as 'non-mothers', and all these writers confront in their own ways issues of lack/absence/refusal involved in choosing, or reconciling oneself to, a life without children. Sheila Heti suggests those without children may 'seem stalled in one place – a place the parents have left behind',[34] and often literary childless/free characters seem disengaged with life's great dramas. The hackneyed image of the witch recurs in many of these texts, suggesting (even if ironically) lives that are lived outside the norm with a potentially destructive impact. Sarah Blau's suggestion that childless detectives Hercule Poirot and Miss Marple – instead of leaving their own trace – track the trace left by someone else, is a poignant reminder of the marginal position of so many childfree literary figures who exist outside family structures and therefore have to find a reason to live and create an alternative legacy to children. Sheila Heti's idea that giving birth to a child is a way of honouring your mother, and the fury unleashed by Margaret Forster's Rosemary at having to attend to her mother's version of her life, indicate how much women remain in thrall to those mothers. As Sarah Blau's narrator warns, 'you never stop being mummy's baby'.[35]

But as feminist thought and action have given new voice to childless/free women's concerns, fiction has moved away from the grey dullness and despair of earlier writing. Now there is an expanded vision of family, friendships and community in which childless and childfree women can play a significant role. Women with creative lives – writers, painters, academics and so on – have always had resources to counter the absence of children. Yet for many women writers and

223

readers, the brutal fact is that if you are not an artist and/or have no big plan or idea, what legacy can you claim and what value are you to a pronatalist society? Well, you are probably using fewer of the world's resources, you are freer to support hard-pressed parents and neglected children, and you have the right to enjoy many experiences without the considerable financial, time-consuming and emotional ties of children and grandchildren. Your legacy is your own life.

Notes

Preface

1   See the most comprehensive study to date of childfreeness (though mainly US-focused): Amy Blackstone, *Childfree by Choice: The Movement Redefining Family and Creating a New Age of Independence* (New York: Dutton, 2019).

2   Duncan Macmillan, 'Thoughts on Lungs', 11 October 2019, https://www.oldvictheatre.com/stories/duncan-macmillan-some-thoughts-on-lungs/.

3   Eva Wiseman, 'Having kids increases global warming. But don't blame the parents . . .', *Guardian*, 13 December 2020, https://www.theguardian.com/lifeandstyle/2020/dec/13/having-kids-increases-global-warming-but-dont-blame-parents.

4   Meehan Crist, 'Is it OK to have a child?', *London Review of Books*, Vol. 42, No. 5, 5 March 2020, https://www.lrb.co.uk/the-paper/v42/n05/meehan-crist/is-it-ok-to-have-a-child.

Chapter 1: Why I Chose a Childfree Life

1   Sheila Heti, *Motherhood* (London: Vintage, 2018), p. 144.

2   Carol Dyhouse, *Love Lives: From Cinderella to Frozen* (Oxford: Oxford University Press, 2021), pp. 105–06.

3   Jodi Picoult, *A Spark of Light* (London: Hodder & Stoughton, 2018), p. 299.

4   Annie Ernaux, *Happening* (London: Fitzcarraldo Editions, 2022), p. 74.

5   Elif Batuman, in 'Prejudice Rules: LRB contributors on the overturning of Roe v. Wade', *London Review of Books*, Vol. 44, No. 14, 21 July 2022, p. 7.

6   Arianne Shahvisi, ibid., p. 16.

7   Linda Geddes, 'Grandmothers may be more connected to grandchildren than to own offspring', *Guardian*, 17 November 2021, https://www.theguardian.com/lifeandstyle/2021/nov/17/grandmothers-may-be-more-connected-to-grandchildren-than-to-own-offspring.

8   Elizabeth Taylor, *The Devastating Boys and Other Stories* (London: Virago, 1984), p. 33.

Chapter 2: Who are 'Our' Children and Grandchildren?

1   Greta Thunberg: 'They see us as a threat because we're having an impact', *Guardian*, 21 July 2019, https://www.theguardian.com/culture/2019/jul/21/greta-thunberg-you-ask-the-questions-see-us-as-a-threat.

2   Geoff Dyer, 'Over and Out', in Meghan Daum, (ed.), *Selfish, Shallow, and Self-Absorbed: Sixteen Writers on the Decision NOT to have kids* (New York: Picador, 2015), p. 200.

3   Arwa Mahdawi, 'No children, no vote: Fox News's latest asinine suggestion', *Guardian*, 31 July 2021, https://www.theguardian.com/commentisfree/2021/jul/31/fox-news-jd-vance-childless-left-week-in-patriarchy.

4   Kate Mosse, *An Extra Pair of Hands: A Story of Caring, Ageing and Everyday Acts of Love* (London: Profile Books, 2021).

5 Chimamanda Ngozi Adichie, *Notes on Grief* (London: 4th Estate, 2021).

6 Anon, 'My Idea of an Ideal Christmas', *The Quiver*, Vol. 53, No. 2, 1917, pp. 115–8, quoted in Kate Macdonald, 'Home is Where the Art Is: Rose Macaulay's Resistance to Domesticity', *Women: A Cultural Review*, Vol. 31, No. 4 (2020), p. 417.

7 Olivia Laing, *To the River: A Journey Beneath the Surface* (Edinburgh: Canongate, 2011), pp. 66 and 107.

Chapter 3: How to find Meaning and Legacy in a Childfree Life

1 Jody Day, *Living the Life Unexpected: How to Find Hope, Meaning and a Fulfilling Future Without Children* (London: Bluebird, 2013).

2 Jody Day, Keynote Lecture, 'Lessons from a Decade of Healing', Childless Collective Summit, 21 March 2021.

3 Shani Silver interviews Jody Day, 'The Single Serving Podcast', January 2021.

4 Day, *Living the Life Unexpected*, pp. 153–55.

5 Jennifer Aniston, 'For the Record', *Huffington Post*, 12 July 2016, quoted in Julie Rodgers, 'On the Margins of Motherhood: Choosing to Be Childfree', in Lucie Joubert's *L'Envers du Landau* (2010), *Women: A Cultural Review*, Vol. 29, No. 1, p. 77; Ann Patchett, interviewed by Emma Barnett, BBC Radio 4 *Woman's Hour*, 3 January 2022, referring to the essay 'There Are No Children Here', in *These Precious Days* (London: Bloomsbury, 2021).

6 Hilary Mantel, email to Helen Taylor, 1 August 2021.

7 Emma John, 'Why are increasing numbers of women choosing to be single?', *Guardian*, 17 January 2021, https://www.theguardian.com/lifeandstyle/2021/jan/17/why-are-increasing-numbers-of-women-choosing-to-be-single.

8   Madeline Miller, *Circe* (London: Bloomsbury, 2018), p. 61.

9   John, 'Why are increasing numbers of women choosing to be single?'

10   Katie Englehart, '"My body is unserviceable and well past its sell-by date": the last days of Avril Henry', *Guardian*, 9 March 2021, https://www.theguardian.com/news/2021/mar/09/the-last-days-of-avril-henry-right-to-die.

11   Tania Hershman, *Who Will Call Me Beloved?*, BBC Radio 4, 11 November 2019, https://www.bbc.co.uk/programmes/m000b4r1.

12   Bernardine Evaristo, *Manifesto: On Never Giving Up* (London: Hamish Hamilton, 2021), pp. 62–3, 63, 186.

13   Hilary Mantel, email to Helen Taylor, 1 August 2021.

14   Amanda Revell Walton, 'Why I'm GLAD I could never be a mum', *Daily Mail*, 10 November 2021, p. 30

Chapter 5: My Family of Friends

1   Danielle Henderson, 'Save Yourself', in Daum, *Selfish, Shallow, and Self-Absorbed*, p.160; Bella DePaulo, *Single, No Children: Who is Your Family?* (Amazon Digital Services: Double-Door Books, 2016); Susie Boyt, 'The sweet return of friendship', *Financial Times,* 28 August 2021 https://www.ft.com/content/65fef7a3-a990-4867-8c7d-8f89e5140ae7.

2   Isabel Allende writes about a similar dream of communal living, but claims she and her friends keep postponing it because of cost, but also 'because deep inside we believe we will always be independent. Magical thinking.' See *The Soul of a Woman* (London: Bloomsbury Circus, 2020), p. 89.

3   Sheila Rowbotham, *Daring to Hope: My Life in the 1970s* (London: Verso, 2021). See especially chapters 10 and 11, pp. 191–241.

4   Kate Christensen, 'A Thousand Other Things', in Daum, *Selfish, Shallow, and Self-Absorbed*, p. 49.

5   The Marxist Feminist Literature Collective, 'Women's Writing: Jane Eyre, Shirley, Villette, Aurora Leigh', in Francis Barker, *et al.*, *1848: The Sociology of Literature: Proceedings of the Essex Conference on the Sociology of Literature*, (Colchester: University of Essex, 1978), pp. 185–206.

6   The Bristol Women's Studies Group, *Half the Sky: An Introduction to Women's Studies* (London: Virago, 1979).

7   Julia Samuel, *Grief Works: Stories of Life, Death and Surviving* (London: Penguin Life, 2017).

Chapter 6: Being Mothered

1   Philip Larkin, 'This Be the Verse,' in *High Windows* (London: Faber & Faber, 1974).

2   Allende, *The Soul of a Woman*, pp. 19–20.

3   See Simone de Beauvoir, *Memoirs of a Dutiful Daughter* (London: André Deutsch and Weidenfeld & Nicolson, 1959); Deborah Orr, *Motherwell: A Girlhood* (London: Orion, 2021).

4   Diana Athill, *Somewhere Towards the End* (London: Granta, 2008), pp. 66 and 67.

Chapter 7: Non-Biological Mothers

1   John Crace, 'Pageantry and queueing collide right on Britain's sweet spot', *Guardian*, 15 September 2022, https://www.theguardian.com/politics/2022/sep/15/if-britain-has-a-tradition-its-in-our-ability-to-talk-about-queueing.

2   *Grayson's Art Club: The Exhibition Volume II* (Bristol Museum and Art Gallery, 2021).

3   Adrienne Rich, *Of Woman Born: Motherhood as Experience and Institution* (London: Virago, 1977), p. 250, quoting Evelyn Reed, *Woman's Evolution: From Matriarchal Clan to Patriarchal Family* (1975). Later quotations come from this book.

4   Ibid., p. 252.

5   Ibid., p. 12.

6   Lillian Smith, quoted in Rich, p. 254.

7   Alice Randall, *The Wind Done Gone* (Boston: Houghton Mifflin, 2001); Toni Morrison, *Beloved* (London: Chatto and Windus, 1987); Damon Galgut, *The Promise* (London: Chatto and Windus, 2021).

8   Quoted in Margo Jefferson, *Constructing a Nervous System: A Memoir* (London: Granta, 2022), p. 168.

9   Yves Denéchère, 'Josephine Baker's "Rainbow Tribe" and the pursuit of universal brotherhood', *The Conversation*, 30 November 2021, https://theconversation.com/josephine-bakers-rainbow-tribe-and-the-pursuit-of-universal-brotherhood-172714.

10   Jefferson, *Constructing a Nervous System*, p.182.

11   Lorna Sage, *Bad Blood: A Memoir* (London: Fourth Estate, 2000), p. 120.

12   Lucy Worsley, 'I would do anything to encourage an INTEREST IN THE PAST!', *Good Housekeeping*, February 2022, p. 13.

13   Louisa Young, '"I avoid them whenever possible": the children's authors who don't like kids', *Guardian*, 13 August 2022, https://www.theguardian.com/society/2022/aug/13/i-avoid-them-whenever-possible-the-childrens-authors-who-dont-like-kids.

14   Allende, *The Soul of a Woman*, p. 148.

15   Pilita Clark, 'Parental leave for pets? We need paws for thought', *i*, 28 October 2021, p. 25.

16   *i*, 26 August 2022, p. 2.

17 Emma Shacklock, 'The Queen's corgis' luxurious lifestyle including "private jet" trips to Windsor and silver dog bowls', *Woman and Home*, 24 August 2022, https://www.womanandhome.com/life/royal-news/the-queens-corgis-luxurious-lifestyle-including-private-jet-trips-to-windsor-and-silver-dog-bowls/.

18 'Choosing pets over babies is "selfish and diminishes us", says pope', *Guardian*, 5 January 2022, https://www.theguardian.com/world/2022/jan/05/pope-couples-choose-pets-children-selfish

19 Simon Kelner, 'Pets make us better people – it's a spiritual experience', *i*, 12 January 2022, p. 22.

Conclusion: Childless by Choice – What does it Mean?

1 Sophie Lewis, *Abolish the Family: A Manifesto for Care and Liberation* (London and New York: Verso, 2022), pp. 57, 85, 83, 84.

2 Katie Grant, 'Cost of living crisis puts dreams of having children out of reach for many', *i*, 4 January 2023, p. 4.

3 Danny Dorling, 'Don't panic about the birth of Baby 8 Billion. Before he's 65 our numbers will be in reverse', *Guardian*, 20 November 2022, https://www.theguardian.com/commentisfree/2022/nov/20/dont-panic-about-birth-baby-8-million-before-hes-65-numbers-will-be-in-reverse

4 Quoted in *Private Eye*, 2–15 December 2022, p. 11.

5 Rebecca Reid, 'Women are going on baby strike', *i*, 2 November 2024, p. 31.

6 Adrienne Rich, 'Motherhood: The Contemporary Emergency and the Quantum Leap' (1978), in *On Lies, Secrets, and Silence: Selected Prose 1966–1978* (New York City: W. W. Norton & Company), p. 269.

7 Zoe Williams, 'The Tory minister's "bonking for Britain" idea is a vile vision lurking behind cheeky Carry On imagery', *Guardian*, 10 October 2022, https://www.theguardian.com/

politics/commentisfree/2022/oct/10/the-tory-ministers-bonking-for-britain-idea-is-a-vile-vision-lurking-behind-cheeky-carry-on-imagery

8   Stella Creasy, 'Rishi Sunak – if you're serious about fixing the British economy, invest in childcare', *Guardian*, 28 October 2022, https://www.theguardian.com/commentisfree/2022/oct/28/rishi-sunak-fixing-british-economy-invest-in-childcare.

9   Maxine Davies, 'The pram in the hall', *Mslexia*, Dec/Jan/Feb 2024/25, p. 13.

10 Tim Kreider, 'The End of the Line', in Daum, *Selfish, Shallow, and Self-Absorbed*, pp. 272–3.

11 Rich, 'The Contemporary Emergency and the Quantum Leap,' p. 272.

Afterword: Literary Childfree Women

1   Although I have long been a teacher and researcher of North American literature, because this book focuses mainly on the UK, most of my examples in this chapter are by British writers.

2   Sigrid Nunez, 'The Most Important Thing', in Daum, *Selfish, Shallow, and Self-Absorbed*, p. 105.

3   George Gissing, *The Odd Women* (New York: Norton, 1977), p. 37.

4   Marjorie Grant, *Latchkey Ladies* (Bath: Handheld Press, 2022), p. 108.

5   Sarah Lefanu, 'Introduction', in Grant, *Latchkey Ladies*, p. xvi.

6   Sylvia Townsend Warner, *Lolly Willowes* (London: The Women's Press, 1978), pp. 6, 97, 169, 234–5, 237.

7   Virginia Woolf, *To the Lighthouse* (London: Penguin, 1964), pp. 23, 58, 120–1, 172, 198–9.

8   Leonard Woolf, (ed.), *A Writer's Diary* (London: Triad/Panther

Books, 1953), pp. 120–2. I am grateful to Maggie Humm for relevant Woolf references.

9   Maggie Humm, *Talland House* (Berkeley, CA: She Writes Press, 2020), pp. 247, 328, 329.

10 Alexander McCall Smith, 'Introduction', in Barbara Pym, *Excellent Women* (London: Virago, 2009), pp. vii, viii–ix, x, xii.

11 George Eliot, *Middlemarch* (Harmondsworth: Penguin, 1965), p. 896.

12 Pym, *Excellent Women*, pp. 113, 180.

13 McCall Smith, 'Introduction', in Pym, *Excellent Women*, p. x.

14 Pym, *Excellent Women*, pp. 3, 94, 249, 288.

15 Barbara Pym, *Quartet in Autumn* (London: Virago, 2015), pp. 71, 3, 186, 56–7.

16 Hilary Mantel, 'Introduction', in Elizabeth Taylor, *Angel* (London: Virago, 2011), p. 2.

17 Taylor, *Angel*, p. 232.

18 Elizabeth Taylor, *Mrs Palfrey at the Claremont* (London: Virago, 1982), pp. 98, 92, 172.

19 Margaret Forster, *Private Papers* (London: Penguin, 1987), pp. 88, 252.

20 Penelope Lively, *Spiderweb* (London: Penguin, 1998), pp. 15, 67.

21 Margaret Drabble, *The Dark Flood Rises* (London: Canongate, 2016), pp. 106, 228–9.

22 Quoted by Lynne Barber, 'Rachel Cusk: A fine contempt', *Guardian*, 30 August 2009, https://www.theguardian.com/books/2009/aug/30/rachel-cusk-lynn-barber.

23 Rachel Cusk, *A Life's Work* (London: Faber and Faber, 2008), pp. 51, 9, 136, 139, 142, 143.

24 Deborah Levy, *Things I Don't Want to Know* (London: Notting Hill Editions, 2013), pp. 13, 14, 15.

25 Ann Patchett, *The Dutch House* (New York: Harper, 2019), pp. 238, 333, 334.

26 Ann Patchett, *These Precious Days* (London: Bloomsbury, 2021), pp. 130, 143, 132, 143.

27 Emma Gannon, *Olive* (London: HarperCollins, 2020), pp. 246, 402.

28 Heti, *Motherhood*, pp. 21, 188, 23, 32, 82–3, 200.

29 Sarah Blau, *The Others*, (trans.) Daniella Zamir (London: Pushkin Press, 2022), pp. 107, 126, 92, 203, 239.

30 Sally Rooney, *Beautiful World, Where Are You* (London: Faber & Faber, 2021), p. 186, 334.

31 Toni Morrison, *Sula* (London: Granada Publishing, 1982), pp. 85, 128, 129.

32 Diana Athill, *Somewhere Towards the End* (London: Granta, 2008), pp. 163, 165, 166.

33 Kate Chopin, *The Awakening* (London: The Women's Press, 1978), p. 188.

34 Heti, *Motherhood*, p. 161.

35 Blau, *The Others*, p. 208.

Further Reading

Chimamanda Ngozi Adichie, *Notes on Grief*, London: 4th Estate, 2021.

Diana Athill, *Somewhere Towards the End*, London: Granta, 2008.

Amy Blackstone, *Childfree by Choice: The Movement Redefining Family and Creating a New Age of Independence*, New York: Dutton, 2019.

Sarah Blau, *The Others*, London: Pushkin Press, 2022.

The Bristol Women's Studies Group, *Half the Sky: An Introduction to Women's Studies*, London: Virago, 1979.

Kate Chopin, *The Awakening*, London: The Women's Press, 1978.

Rachel Cooke, *The Virago Book of Friendship*, London: Virago, 2024.

Rhiannon Lucy Cosslett, *The Year of the Cat: A Love Story*, London: Headline, 2023.

Rachel Cusk, *A Life's Work: On Becoming a Mother*, London: Faber & Faber, 2008.

Jody Day, *Living the Life Unexpected: How to Find Hope, Meaning and a Fulfilling Future Without Children*, London, Bluebird, 2013.

Meghan Daum, (ed.), *Selfish, Shallow, and Self-Absorbed: Sixteen Writers on the Decision NOT to Have Kids,* New York: Picador, 2015.

Margaret Drabble, *The Dark Flood Rises*, London: Canongate, 2016.

Stella Duffy, *Lullaby Beach*, London: Virago, 2020.

Carol Dyhouse, *Love Lives: From Cinderella to Frozen*, Oxford: Oxford University Press, 2021.

Annie Ernaux, *Happenings*, London: Fitzcarraldo Editions, 2022.

Bernardine Evaristo, *Manifesto: On Never Giving Up*, London: Hamish Hamilton, 2021.

Margaret Forster, *Hidden Lives: A Family Memoir*, London: Penguin, 1996.

Margaret Forster, *Private Papers*, London: Penguin, 1987.

Emma Gannon, *Olive*, London: HarperCollins, 2020.

George Gissing, *The Odd Women* (1893), New York: Norton, 1977.

Marjorie Grant, *Latchkey Ladies*, Bath: Handheld Press, 2022.

Sheila Heti, *Motherhood*, London: Vintage, 2018.

Maggie Humm, *Talland House*, Berkeley, CA: She Writes Press, 2020.

Rosie Jackson, *Mothers Who Leave: Behind the Myth of Women Without Their Children*, London: Harper Collins, 1994.

Rosie Jackson, *The Glass Mother: A Memoir*, Norwich and London: Unthank Books, 2016.

Nina Jervis, *I'd Rather Get a Cat and Save the Planet: Conversations with Childfree Women*, Nina the Writer, 2020.

Olivia Laing, *To the River: A Journey Beneath the* Surface, Edinburgh: Canongate, 2011.

Deborah Levy, *Things I Don't Want to Know*, London: Notting Hill Editions, 2013.

Penelope Lively, *Spiderweb*, London: Penguin, 1998.

Hilary Mantel, *Giving Up the Ghost: A Memoir*, London: Fourth Estate, 2003.

Toni Morrison, *Sula* (1973), London: Chatto & Windus, 1982.

Kate Mosse, *An Extra Pair of Hands: A Story of Caring, Ageing and Everyday Acts of Love*, London: Profile Books, 2021.

Deborah Orr, *Motherwell: A Girlhood*, London: Orion, 2021.

Ann Patchett, *These Precious Days*, London: Bloomsbury, 2021.

Ann Patchett, *The Dutch House*, New York: Harper, 2019.

Jodi Picoult, *A Spark of Light*, London: Hodder & Stoughton, 2018.

Barbara Pym, *Excellent Women* (1952), London: Virago, 2009.

Barbara Pym, *Quartet in Autumn* (1977), London: Virago, 2015.

Alice Randall, *The Wind Done Gone*, Boston: Houghton Mifflin, 2001.

Adrienne Rich, *Of Women Born: Motherhood as Experience and Institution*, London: Virago, 1977.

Sally Rooney, *Beautiful World, Where Are You*, London: Faber & Faber, 2021.

Sheila Rowbotham, *Daring to Hope: My Life in the 1970s*, London: Verso, 2021.

Elizabeth Taylor, *Mrs Palfrey at the Claremont* (1971), London: Virago, 1982.

Elizabeth Taylor, *The Devastating Boys and Other Stories*, London: Virago, 1984.

Elizabeth Taylor, *Angel* (1957), London: Virago, 2011.

Helen Taylor, *Scarlett's Women: Gone With the Wind and its Female Fans*, London: Virago, 1989, reprinted 2014.

Helen Taylor, *Why Women Read Fiction: The Stories of Our Lives*, Oxford: Oxford University Press, 2019.

Sylvia Townsend Warner, *Lolly Willowes*, London: The Women's Press, 1978.

Ruby Warrington, *Women Without Kids: The Revolutionary Rise of an Unsung Sisterhood*, London: Orion Spring, 2023.

Virginia Woolf, *To the Lighthouse* (1927), London: Penguin, 1964.

Acknowledgements

This is the most personal book I've ever written, and I am grateful to my family and friends for encouraging and supporting me while it took shape. Many important people in my life are no longer here, but I hope they would have approved of the way I've discussed them and used their material – especially my mother Ida. There are so many friends who have shared ideas and comments with me, including Stef Brammar, Sarah Dunant, Richard Dyer, Judith Glushanok, Maggie Humm, Margaret Kirkham, Alison Light, Janet Reibstein, Sue Swingler, and Pauline Trudell (forgive any omissions). I am indebted to the women – mostly anonymous or pseudonymous – who shared their experiences of childfreeness with me via email, and I'm sad to have space to quote only a few.

I've benefitted from comments on early draft chapters of the book by Anne Finlay-Baird, Lesley Murphy and Anthea Callen. Sarah LeFanu read the whole manuscript, making some invaluable suggestions for improvement.

I appreciated the enthusiasm of my agent Elizabeth Sheinkman, who recommended me to John Bond at Whitefox, and I've been grateful to him and to Julia Koppitz for their warmly supportive help with producing this book. My copyeditor Gemma Wain did a splendid job finding inconsistencies and repetitions. Nigel Lambert generously constructed my website and has kept a close caretaking eye on it ever since.

As ever, my greatest debt is to Derrick Price (DJ in the book) who – throughout our childfree life together – has supported and cared for me, and brought me much comfort and joy.

About the Author

Helen Taylor has published books on women's writing, American southern culture and women fiction readers. Her latest much-acclaimed work is *Why Women Read Fiction: The Stories of Our Lives*. Her best-known works focus on popular writing and culture: *Scarlett's Women: Gone With the Wind and its Female Fans*, *The Daphne du Maurier Companion* and *Circling Dixie: Contemporary Southern Culture through a Transatlantic Lens*.

She taught English and American literature at three universities – West of England, Warwick and Exeter, where she was Head of English and is now Emeritus Professor. She has published widely on the literature and culture of the American South, as well as British and American women's writing. For many years, she has been a Chair, Curator and participant in many literary festivals, including Bath, Cheltenham, Oxford, Fowey, Budleigh Salterton and Clifton, and she was the first Director of the Liverpool Literature Festival. She is currently writing a book on Daphne du Maurier for the series 'Writers and Their Works'. She lives in Bristol.

www.ingramcontent.com/pod-product-compliance
Ingram Content Group UK Ltd.
Pitfield, Milton Keynes, MK11 3LW, UK
UKHW012027110625
6352UKWH00002B/6

9 781917 523301